Salzburg and the Jews:
A Historical Walking Guide

Stan Nadel

Edited by Will Deming

WIPF & STOCK · Eugene, Oregon

Wipf and Stock Publishers
199 W 8th Ave, Suite 3
Eugene, OR 97401

Salzburg and the Jews
A historical walking guide
By Nadel, Stan
Copyright©2005 Jung und Jung, Salzburg und Wien Alle Rechte vorbehalten
ISBN 13: 978-1-60608-593-6
Publication date 3/16/2009
Previously published by Jung und Jung, Salzburg und Wien Alle Rechte vorbehalten, 2005

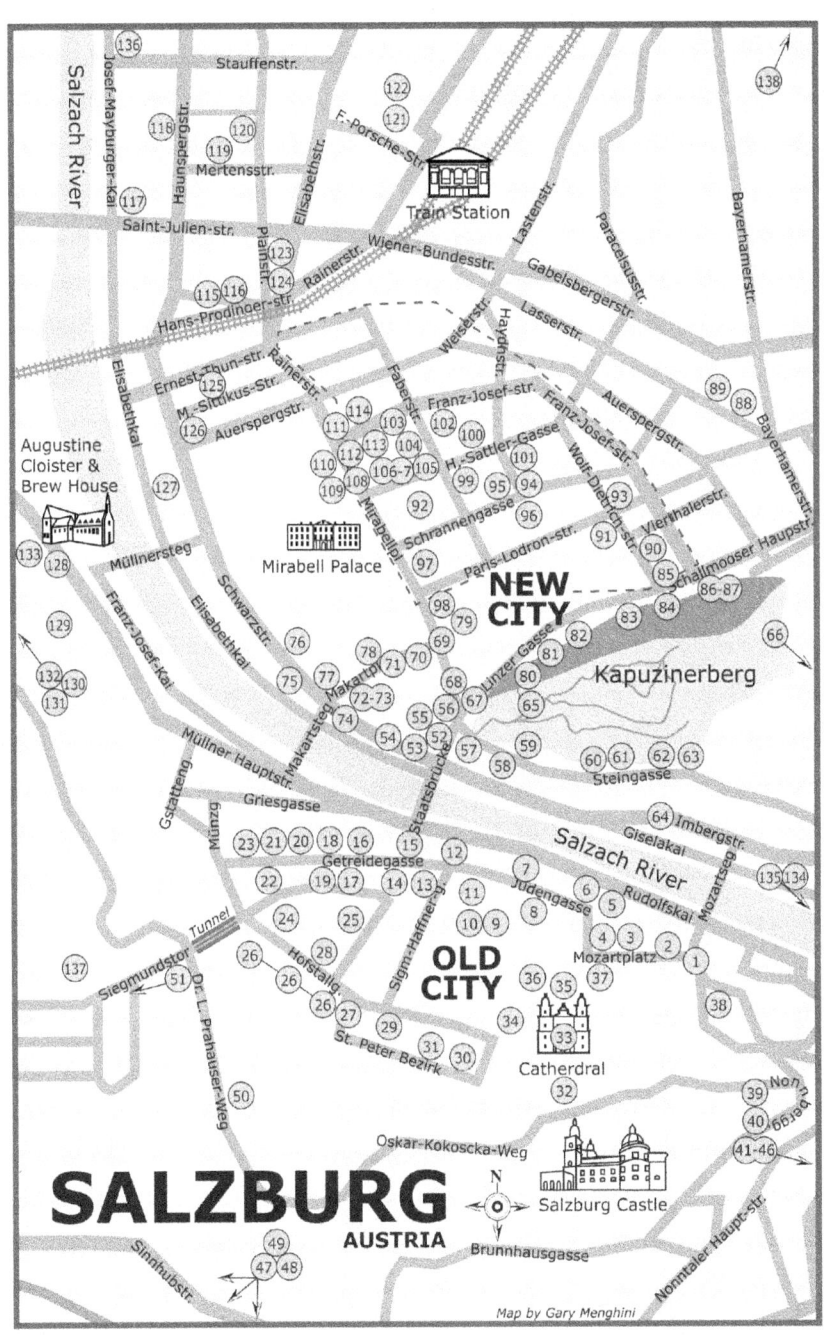

Contents

Map of Salzburg 1

Preface 5

Introduction 7

Historical Overview 8

Part I: The Old City 9

Part II: Across the River and Back Again 63

Part III: Some Additional Sites 137

Organizations of Interest with Contact Information 138

Bibliography 139

Notes 140

Index of Entries 141

Preface

When I moved to Salzburg in 2002 I followed in the footsteps of thousands of others and fell in love with this quaint old city and its beautiful surroundings. I am a historian by trade and I was enchanted with walking the city's streets and identifying where various historical events had taken place. I am also Jewish, so I read all I could about the history of Jews in Salzburg and began to fit what I learned into the geography of the streets and buildings that I so much enjoyed. As I learned more about the city and its history, I found it unsettling to see the shadows of a very ugly past in the city I have come to love. I liked my first apartment, but I was not happy that one of Adolf Eichmann's associates lived in an apartment downstairs after it had been taken away from an elderly Jewish man.

When it was necessary for me to move, I found a new apartment that I really love—but I learned that the whole building had been taken away from a Jewish family in 1938. There are many such shadows in Salzburg, but it remains a beautiful city with many attractions. I certainly do not want to discourage anyone from coming to Salzburg to enjoy, as I do, its beauty, culture, food and wonderful beers. To the contrary, I would like to encourage others to come and share my pleasure. But I also want to share what I have learned with visitors to Salzburg who might like to know about some aspects of its history that are often neglected by the standard tourist guidebooks.

◆◆◆

This guide would not have been possible without the hard work of numerous historians whose publications have provided me with the resources I needed to create it—and I wish to publicly express my gratitude. Most important were the works of Rabbi Dr. Adolf Altmann, Thomas Albrich, Heinz Dopsch, Helga Embacher, Günter Fellner, Ernst Hanisch, Robert Hoffmann, Gert Kerschbaumer, Dan Leeson, Walter Leitner, and Albert Lichtblau. The work of Jewish Community leader Marko Feingold has also been of invaluable assistance, both to the Jewish Community and to preserving the history I have related here. I also want to thank Dr. Sabine Veits-Falk of the Salzburg City Archives, for her enthusiastic help in getting further information about numerous topics and leading me to materials I would never have thought to ask for, along with Robert Hoffmann, Helga Embacher and Ernst Hanisch, for reading and commenting on earlier drafts of this work. Being able to discuss this material with Sylvia Hahn was invaluable; her suggestions and contributions improved this work considerably and it would not have been possible at all without her love and support. My thanks too to Will Deming for suggesting that the University of Portland Press undertake this edition, and for his editorial work on this English version. While all of these good people deserve most of the credit for those things I have gotten right, any mistakes are my own.

Introduction

This book is a supplement to, rather than a substitute for, the standard tourist guides. It is mostly a guide to Salzburg's Jewish history, but it extends to other parts of Salzburg's history that strike me as somehow related. Thus, it covers mostly sites associated with Antisemitism and Nazis, but also some sites associated with other aspects of Salzburg's history that resonate with the Jewish experience here. The guide is organized into two long walking tours of different parts of the city, and the entries are ordered to accommodate walking tours, rather than following the numbers of the street addresses. There is also a map to help the reader see how the sites relate to the larger city, and photographs intended to highlight the shadows of the past even if I cannot bring the past to life.

Historical Overview

The history of Jews in Salzburg will be developed through the entries in this guide, but a short overview is in order first. Jews have lived in Salzburg since at least the middle of the 1200s, though it is possible that some Jews may have lived in the Roman city that was founded here more than a thousand years earlier. It is a long, but not an easy history. A small settlement of Jewish merchants became established in the 1200s and grew into a real community over the next century, only to be wiped out around 1350 when the Black Death struck Europe and the plague was blamed on the Jews. A Jewish Salzburg was re-founded in the 1370s, and the second community lasted until the great Salzburg Jew burning of 1404. A third community was founded by 1418 and prospered for a while, but it had dwindled to a shadow of its mid-century size before it was expelled in 1498.

Jews were basically excluded from living in Salzburg for the next 360 years, though some converts were able to live here—like Emanuel David, a Catholic Priest who in 1852 became the founding editor of Salzburg's *Catholic Church-Newspaper* (*Katholischen Kirchenblatt*). A fourth Salzburg Jewish community was founded in the last third of the nineteenth century, which grew and flourished in the face of growing Antisemitism until the Nazis took power, first in Germany (1933) and then in Austria (1938). By late 1938 Salzburg's Nazi leaders declared that all Jews had been driven out of Salzburg, but that was an exaggeration and it is not clear that Salzburg was ever really without any Jews during the Nazi years.

After the Nazis were defeated in 1945 Salzburg became a major center for Jewish refugees leaving Europe, mostly en route to Palestine (or "Israel," after 1948). A few of Salzburg's pre-1938 Jews returned after the war and some of the thousands of Jewish refugees stayed to re-establish a Jewish community here. Today Salzburg has a small Jewish community with somewhere over one hundred Jews living in the city and its environs, and it has both a synagogue and a prayer house in the Hassidic, *Chabad* tradition.

Part I

◆◆◆

The Old City

1. *Mozart Square (Mozartplatz)*: Any consideration of Jewish Salzburg has to open with the Roman city, *Civitas Claudia Juvavum*, established here by the Emperor Claudius in the year 50 CE. *Juvavum* was strategically located where the main north-south road crossed the river. The road from the south followed the east bank because of the swamps on the west side of the river, while the road north followed the west bank to avoid the swampy area north of the *Kapuzinerberg* (Capuchins' Mountain). Salzburg was also the place where this north-south road met an important route headed east (now called the *Linzergasse*).

There is no record of any Jewish community in *Juvavum*, but there were Jewish communities in Roman towns like *Trier* along the Rhine and there was one in Graz by 70 CE. As *Juvavum* was on the main trade route between the two areas, Jews must have passed through when traveling between them and some may even have lived here at some time. Roman *Juvavum* was at least as large as medieval Salzburg, and the remains of a good size Roman temple were found near *Linzergasse*. Like the medieval town, *Juvavum* extended east along the road under the north side of *Kapuzinerberg*. It flourished for two hundred years, and then struggled along for some centuries after that. A spectacular Roman mosaic was found on this site when the foundation for the Mozart memorial statue was excavated in the nineteenth century. The statue was later the scene of a series of Nazi ceremonies as they tried to appropriate Mozart for their cause (see §17).

Commemoration of the 150th anniversary of Mozart's death in 1941 by officials and members of the Hitler Youth at Mozart Square.

---

2. Mozartplatz 5 — Memorial Plaque for Theodor Herzl: Theodor Herzl, the founder of modern Zionism, came to Salzburg when he was a young man. After he got his law degree in 1884 he needed to serve an internship before he could get a job as a lawyer, and many years later he wrote that he sought a position with a judge in Salzburg because "the scenery around the city was famous for its beauty." Like so many others, Herzl was enchanted with the city: "My workroom was in an old fortress tower, directly under the belltower, and three times a day it rang sweetly in my ears…"

His recollections continue with the words inscribed on this memorial plaque "I spent some of the happiest hours of my life in Salzburg. I would have gladly stayed in that beautiful city, but as a Jew I would never have been able to gain a judicial position. On this account I abandoned Salzburg and legal studies." (Other evidence suggests that Herzl, in fact, disliked his law career, and that it was his ambition to become a writer that led him to abandon provincial

Salzburg for Vienna.)

Marko Feingold, a Holocaust survivor, was also taken with the beauty of Salzburg. He arrived here in 1945 and he stayed on to become the long-term leader of the Jewish Community. Herzl's words about the beauty of Salzburg caught his imagination and he got the local authorities to put up this memorial plaque in 2000. Focusing on the positive, Feingold wanted the plaque to quote only the part of Herzl's statement about his happy times in Salzburg, but the rest of the text was added when some activists charged that the city was trying to cover up an unseemly part of its past. (For more on Feingold, see §133.)

3. Waagplatz: Salzburg's roots in the Middle Ages go back both to the surviving remnants of Roman *Juvavum* that clung to the slopes of the Castle hill, and to the establishment of Salzburg as an outpost of the emerging kingdom of the Franks. As early as 996 Salzburg's archbishops were granted some market rights, which began the development of a town outside the archbishop's palace walls. Jews were numerous along the Rhine at the start of the second millennium and started moving out of the Rhineland after the First Crusade pogroms of 1096-1099. Some of them came into this region, including, in 1130, to the village of *Judendorf* (Jews' Village). Located in the Austrian province of *Styria*, and now called *Judenburg*, this town was then in the Salzburg Archbishopric.

The establishment of the market by the gate outside the Residence increasingly attracted business. Among others, the market attracted Jews who were active in the wine and other trades. Originally called the *Marktplatz* (Market Square), it is now known as the *Waagplatz*, "*Waage*" being the scales used by merchants for weighing merchandise. For a time it was also known as the *Heumarkt* (Haymarket), after the main market was moved to a larger space near the bridge, around 1300.

Even though a Jewish community developed in the town of Salzburg, other Jewish settlements in the area were larger and more important for a long time, especially the one in *Hallein*, nine miles (15 km) to the south. In 1346 Jews were officially granted the right to trade in wine and grain, to keep inns, to own land, and to loan money at interest. They were also permitted to take most forms of property as security, but not arms or armor (though they themselves could carry weapons). The same document gave them the right to a trial before a mixed court (half Jewish, half Christian) in disputes with Christians, and to a purely Jewish court in internal disputes. They also had the right to take oaths on the Torah rather than the Christian Bible. By 1346 things were definitely looking very good for Jews in the Archbishopric of Salzburg.

4. Waagplatz 6: In the 1880s and early 1890s this was the location of the Salzburg branch of Neuburger and Einstein's fabric store. By the middle of the 1890s they had closed their operations in Salzburg in favor of their main store in Munich. Yet, despite growing up in Munich rather than Salzburg, the birthplace of the great composer Wolfgang Mozart, Ludwig Einstein's son Alfred was destined to become one of the most distinguished Mozart scholars of the 20th century.

5. Judengasse (Jews' Street): In the Middle Ages Jews lived close together between the market and the bridge, on the street that has been called *Judengasse* since the 14th Century. *Judengasse* was gated and likely closed off at night, but that seems generally to have been the case with the streets of medieval Salzburg. For that reason it would probably not be correct to consider it a classic ghetto, especially as *Judengasse* was probably not exclusively Jewish.

6. Judengasse 15: This was the original synagogue, known as the *Judenschul* (Jews' School). It is not clear when it was established, though it seems to have been in operation by 1346. But in 1348-49 a devastating disease called the Black Death struck Europe. Most likely, this was Bubonic plague, a disease spread by rats and their fleas.

This new disease killed almost one out of every three Europeans in just a few years. Many Europeans, not knowing what caused the new disease, blamed it on the Jews, though Jews suffered as much from the Black Death as anyone else. It was claimed that Jews had poisoned the wells to cause the plague and kill all the Christians. Jewish communities were attacked all over Central Europe. The exception was Austria, where the ruler Albrecht II ordered their protection. Unfortunately for the Jews of Salzburg, Salzburg was not then in Austria, so they were unprotected by Albrecht's order. These Jews, both in the city and all over the archbishopric, were burned to death in a futile attempt to stop the plague.

Depiction of Jews burned to death in 1349.

Twenty years after the Black Death, Salzburg's new Archbishop, Pilgrim I, began to encourage foreign traders to come into his territory, even offering them special privileges denied to local merchants. By 1370 Jews were back in Salzburg and for the first time the town of Salzburg developed into the major Jewish settlement in the archbishopric. They again specialized in the wine and grain trades, as well as money lending, and in 1376 Christian merchants petitioned the Archbishop to restrict them to money lending. The next year produced the earliest known references to "the *Judengasse*" and to the synagogue near the *Heumarkt* (now *Waagplatz*). Once again things were going well for Jews in Salzburg—so well that in 1382 two armed and mounted Jews from Salzburg were included in the Archbishop's forces fighting on the nearby *Berchtesgaden* frontier against Bavaria.

At the end of the 14th century the Archbishop even sold the property at *Judengasse* 15 to Nahem, Heli, and Eleazer, three representatives of the Jewish community of Salzburg, giving the community ownership of the building which housed the synagogue. Then came the installation of a new Archbishop, Eberhard III. In May of 1404 the new Archbishop confirmed the existing rights and privileges of Jews in Salzburg, including ownership of the synagogue and the right to worship there, in exchange for a substantial payment of 16 Hungarian Gulden per year.

But about a month later, on July 6, a charge of Host desecration (that is, desecration of the consecrated communion wafers used in the Roman Catholic Mass) was raised against the Jews. A thief caught stealing valuables from the *Müllner* Church just north of the town (now part of Salzburg) claimed that he had been paid by the Jews to steal communion wafers so that they could desecrate them in their synagogue. Late medieval Christians believed that this would produce the blood of Christ from the wafers—blood that the Jews would then use in Satanic rituals. As a result, the Jews were rounded up, their synagogue and houses were searched (no communion wafers were found) and some of the men were tortured.

Depiction of an alleged 1338 Host desecration in Austria: Jews torture a communion wafer from the Mass as an accusing angel looks on.

Under torture, two men confessed both to this crime and to having bought a Christian child for the purpose of ritually draining its blood. The allegation that Jews engaged in such a bizarre ritual had originated in Norwich England in 1144, and had quickly spread throughout the Christian world. (In the last two-hundred years, it has been revived and spread to Islamic countries; and it is also current in a significant number of militant Christian and Neo-Nazi groups, as a quick internet search of "ritual murder" will demonstrate.) In this case, the body of a baby (*not* drained of blood) was discovered in the Salzburg Cathedral, possibly left by a guilt-ridden, unwed mother, and that became the basis of the charge. Soon after giving their forced confessions, the two Jewish men committed suicide.

A Jew in the 16th century being tortured by strappado, *or "reverse hanging."*

Despite the flimsiness of the evidence, on July 10, 1404, seventy Jews, comprising all Salzburg Jews over age ten, were burned to death—except for two pregnant women and one wealthy man who converted to Christianity (see §127). The Jews of nearby *Hallein* were also burned to death at this time because they had allegedly gotten communion wafers and Christian blood from the Salzburg Jews. This was not a "pogrom" as some historians have called it; rather it was an official judicial action. The burning of the Jews was presided over by the Archbishop and his brother, who was then rewarded with ownership of the synagogue property at *Judengasse* 15.

Depiction of the rounding up the Jews in Salzburg 1404.
The caption reads: "Because the Jews desecrated the most worthy Sacrament, some were burned and the others were driven from the country."

Four hundred years later, and three hundred years after the so-called "permanent" expulsion of Salzburg's Jews in 1498, Salzburg ceased to be an independent country ruled by its Archbishop. This was a result of the wars that followed the French Revolution and the rise of Napoleon. In the years 1811-12 Salzburg was a province of Napoleonic Bavaria, where Jews were once again permitted to live and trade. As a consequence, some twenty Jewish traders participated in the Salzburg market in those two years, staying in the city's inns. On February 21, 1811, a Jewish trader from Bohemia named Kohn stayed at the *Höllbräu*, an inn that occupied this site for centuries. Only recently has it been taken over by the Radisson Hotels company and renamed the Hotel *Altstadt*. In its later years the *Höllbräu* had a wall-plaque inside commemorating the old synagogue, but it was taken down during the Hotel *Altstadt* renovation and never replaced.

7. *Judengasse 17:* The apartment on the left side of the third floor was the home of the widow Regina "Stella" Grindlinger and her children Henrietta and Tina when Austria was incorporated into Nazi Germany's Third *Reich* through Hitler's "Annexation" (*Anschluss*) of 1938. They were the only Jews known to have been living on *Judengasse* at the time, and the apartment was soon "Aryanized."

The Nazi's "Aryanization" program was devoted to taking all Jewish property (especially apartments, businesses, and houses) and turning it over to "Aryans"—frequently Nazi party members and their friends deemed to be "racially" pure Germans. In this case it was given to a local official named Franz Holzgruber, while the Grindlingers moved to Vienna. Soon afterwards Salzburg claimed the "honor" of being the first city in the Third *Reich* to be "*Judenrein*"—a Nazi term meaning "cleansed of Jews." The director of the "Aryanization" program in Salzburg, Erich Gebert, was a local man who had joined the SS years before the Annexation. He had been an employee of the Chamber of Commerce (*Handelskammer*) since 1921, and he became its president in 1941.

8. *Judengasse 12—the Iron Broom:* In 1919 the "German-Austrian Protection Society and Antisemitic League" was founded in Vienna and began publishing a viciously Antisemitic paper called the *Iron Broom (Der eiserne Besen)*. The Antisemitic League had brought together Antisemites from the Catholic Christian Social Party with old style German Nationalist Antisemites and Nazis. All of these factions were represented in the Antisemitic League's executive council, but Nazis increasingly provided much of the leadership, becoming both the motivating force in the organization of the *Iron Broom* as well as its editors.

The first Salzburg edition of the Iron Broom, *listing Jewish businesses to be boycotted and featuring a story on "Jewish Morality and Ritual Murder."*

In 1921 a Salzburg division of the League was founded and soon became one of its most important branches. In 1923 it took over publication of the *Iron Broom*, moving both the paper and the League's offices here. The Antisemites may or may not have recognized the incongruity of having their headquarters on a street named *Judengasse*, but eventually they moved to a "better" location near St. Peter's. The *Iron Broom*, which was every bit as vicious as the more infamous Nazi paper *Der Stürmer*, was published in Salzburg until 1932.

An Iron Broom *cartoon from 1932: a Nazi chokes a Jew who is spreading the poison gases of speculation, pacifism, Jewish theater, Jewish newspapers, Jewish movies, etc.*

9. The Old Market (Alter Markt): In the early 14th century the main market moved from the *Waagplatz* to a larger area at the other end of *Judengasse* called the *Marktplatz* (Market Square). It was next to the gate by the Medieval bridge over the *Salzach* River, in the same place where the Romans had built their bridge. In the late 19th and early 20th century it was called the *Ludwig-Victor-Platz* after a Habsburg

Archduke; and after the abolition of the Habsburg monarchy at the end of WWI, it became the "Old Market." In the early 20th century this plaza was still the main shopping district in Salzburg, with many large and fine shops.

10. *Alter Markt 12 and Kranzlmarkt 4:* These two buildings constituted Schwarz's Department Store. The business was founded by Samuel Schwarz in 1908 and grew rapidly. On September 19, 1918, a deminstration against shortages caused by the war escalated into an attack on places housing refugees from the war zones, and then turned on Schwarz's and some other shops. (The refugees consisted mostly of non-German Austrians from the Russian front, about 15% of whom were Jewish.) A few weeks later the Catholic Farmers' League paper, the *Salzburg People's News* (*Salzburger Volksbote*) published this call: "Christian German People! Know the danger! Drive the Jews out...You poor German People. We remain Antisemites." Despite the looting of their store and the rising threat of Antisemitism, Samuel's son Walter rebuilt Schwarz's into what became the largest department store in Salzburg by the 1930s.

After the German Annexation of Austria in the spring of 1938, Walter and his two brothers (the three owners) were arrested. Like other imprisoned Jews they had to agree to turn their property and business over to a Nazi administrator in order to obtain release. After a fight between different groups of Nazis over who would get to benefit from the "Aryanization" of Schwarz's store, the bulk of the business was liquidated in 1939, although a portion of the operation was continued in the *Kranzlmarkt* location. What was left of the store was taken over and run by SS man Karl Teinfelt with two partners, Josef Böhm and Alexander Fränzel.

A sign reading "Jewish business" (Judengeschäft) *and an SA Stormtrooper in front of Schwarz's Department Store in 1938.*

The liquidation was carried out by the Salzburg Savings Bank (*Salzburger Sparkasse*), which retained ownership of the properties. In the 1920s the Savings Bank had supported Antisemitic activities by taking out advertising in the *Iron Broom*. Even more vital to its role in the "Aryanization" process, however, was the political make up of the Bank's board that resulted from its ties with the provincial government. These ties meant that when the Nazis took over Salzburg, they also took over the bank leadership.

Two of the three Schwarz brothers, Paul and Max, escaped into exile after their release from *Dachau*. Walter was re-arrested by the *Gestapo* when he tried to join his wife Dora, who had already moved to Palestine. The *Gestapo* men appear to have believed that there was more money to be squeezed out of him and he was hanged in the *Gestapo* headquarters in Munich on September 1, 1939. The *Gestapo* claimed it was suicide. (For more on Walter Schwarz and his family, see §52 and §105.)

Max Schwarz returned to Salzburg in 1949 with Walter's son Hugo to re-establish their business. Initially they were able to regain the portion of the property on *Kranzlmarkt*, but not the larger part on the Old Market; and they were forced to pay the Savings Bank for expensive improvements to the property before they were allowed to resume control. Although it seems that some of the new post-war directors were sincerely anxious to make amends to the Schwarzes, they were unwilling or unable to have the bank take more of a loss on the return of the property.

Following Max's death in 1950, Hugo had little interest in running the store and he turned it over to some cousins, Howard and Thomas Schein in 1954. They renovated and expanded the store back onto the Old Market. But the store did not do well enough to keep the Scheins in Salzburg, especially after the American army left Salzburg in 1955, leaving it with far fewer customers. Howard Schein recalled that many Salzburgers were too Antisemitic to shop there. The prejudice, he said, was so strong that some customers even insisted that their packages be wrapped in unmarked paper so that their neighbors would not know where they had come from. Howard Schein's girlfriend was thrown out by her parents for associating with a Jew, and old Antisemitic rumors circulated around Salzburg that all the salesgirls were forced to go to bed with the Jewish owners. In 1962 the Scheins gave up and sold the store to Bally.

11. *Kranzlmarkt 2–4:* In the 15th century the *Kranzlmarkt* ("Little Garland Market") was known as the Vegetable Market (*Gemüsemarkt*). In 1418, only fourteen years after the second destruction of Salzburg Jewry, the Salzburg Provincial Synod met and passed a set of regulations regarding Jews, indicating that Jews had returned to Salzburg. Jewish men were required to wear a pointed hat (it was called a "horned" hat, which may have contributed to the widespread Christian belief that Jews had horns), and Jewish women were required to wear a bell, like lepers. Salzburg was the only place ever known to have required Jewish women to wear bells.

Jews wearing "horned hats." (A relief from Hallein, near Salzburg, ca. 1600.)

In the 1420s Salzburg looked attractive to many Jewish refugees, due to Jew burnings and mass expulsions from Vienna, the rest of Austria, Prague, and Bohemia. This was especially true after the death of Archbishop Eberhard III in 1429, and Jewish Salzburg revived. The old synagogue and the houses on *Judengasse* were never given back to the Jewish community, and many of the new Jewish residents lived across the river (see §52-63). Even so, they established a new synagogue here at what is now *Kranzlmarkt* 2 and 4.

In 1423 the site was reportedly owned by a rich Venetian merchant and moneychanger who may well have been Jewish, which would explain the location of the synagogue here. Sometime around 1910, Dr. Adolf Altmann, author of the monumental two volume history of the Jews of Salzburg before 1930, visited the cellar of *Kranzlmarkt* 2 and he reported that the old synagogue was still visible down there. He recorded that it was architecturally similar to the famous "Old-New Synagogue" (*Altneusynagogue*) of Prague, which suggests that some of Salzburg's 14th century Jews may well have been refugees from Prague.

Dr. Altmann later learned that the original synagogue extended under what is now *Kranzlmarkt* 4 as well, and that the wall dividing the two basements had been added at a later time. This continued to be Salzburg's synagogue until the expulsion of 1498 (see §40). There were a series of threats against the Jews of Salzburg in the 15th century, especially after the alleged martyrdom of Simon of Trent. This was supposed to have happened in 1475 in Triento, Italy (just across the Alps), at the hands of "the Jews" (—yet another ritual murder charge). But the Jews of Salzburg were able to get an Imperial letter from Friedrich III, reminding the Archbishop that Jews were the Emperor's property and instructing him to protect them as such.

12. *Kranzlmarkt 1—The Town Hall (Rathaus) and the "Jews' Sow" (Judensau)*: Until the death of Emperor Friedrich III in 1493 and the installation of Archbishop Leonhard von Keutschach in 1495, both the Emperor and the Archbishop were committed to protecting the Jews—in exchange for hefty tax payments. Thus the Jew haters of Salzburg found that they could not attack the Jews directly, so they resorted to insult. The Town Hall (*Rathaus*) was built in 1407 and, by order of the Archbishops, it was for centuries the only non-church building in Salzburg allowed to have a tower. In 1486 Mayor Hans Glavenberger and the members of the city council commissioned a well-known sculptor named Hans Valkenauer to carve a marble frieze for the tower. It was a classic "Jews' Sow" (*Judensau*), a picture of Jews sucking at the teats of a female pig; and it was mounted so as to face the *Kranzlmarkt* synagogue.

*A woodcut of the Salzburg "Jews' Sow" (*Judensau*).*

Because this was a challenge to the Archbishop and the Emperor, as well as an insult to the Jews, the frieze was ordered taken down soon after it was installed. But after Archbishop Leonhard von Keutschach ordered the expulsion of the Jews from all of Archbishopric Salzburg in 1498, it was restored to the Town Hall tower at his order. He also ordered the "cleansing" of the synagogues, resorting to a terminology that would later be used by the Nazis. In 1520 the "Jews' Sow" was refurbished and put on a larger clock tower, built in 1616-18. This same renovation added a marble statue of Justice over the Town Hall entrance. The "Jews' Sow" remained there until the 300 year-old offence was ordered removed and destroyed in 1785 by the "Enlightenment" Archbishop, Hieronymus Count Colloredo—the same Archbishop who drove Mozart out of Salzburg!

13. *Sigmund Haffnerstrasse 9:* The Fischer and Aninger shop was here in 1938. It was owned by Emilie and Ludwig Fischer, and Klara and Heinrich Aninger—all Jewish. That year it was "Aryanized" by the Nazis.

14. *Schatz Passage and the Bebel Memorial Plaque:* Over the section of passage connecting the first and second courtyards is a tablet commemorating August Bebel's time in Salzburg. Bebel was a famous German political leader who helped create the German Socialist Party. He lived here in 1859 when he was just a nineteen year-old journeyman wood turner. It was the custom for artisans to travel around and learn additional skills after they finished their apprenticeships (hence "journeymen"),

While in Salzburg, Bebel became friends with Dr. Josef Anton Schöpf, a Catholic priest known for his decades long work with young journeymen and for his campaign against Antisemitism in the 1880s (see §33). When political Antisemitism arose in the late 19th century, focusing its anger on "Jewish capitalism," Bebel famously defined Antisemitism as "the Socialism of fools." Nonetheless, his "fools" took up residence here in 1918 when the newly formed

Salzburg section of the Nazi Party set up its offices on the second floor. This continued to be the Nazi headquarters in Salzburg for many years. In 1936 the anti-Socialist dictatorship then ruling Austria had the memorial plaque commemorating Bebel's residence here taken down. It was restored in 1948.

Before leaving the Schatz passage visitors would do well to stop in at the Konditorei Schatz a few feet away—it is a marvelous old coffee and pastry shop with the best traditional pastries in Salzburg.

15. *Town Hall Square (Rathausplatz)*: In the 14th century this was called the Fish Market (*Fischmarkt*), which was located here because the fishing was especially good in the *Salzach* River outside the gate at the foot of the square. This was immediately downstream from the medieval bridge where animals were butchered and the offal was dumped into the river, so fish were large and numerous here. The Fish Market was also the site of the town well (*Stadtbrunn*). After 1349 this well became known as the "Jews' Well" (*Judenprunn*), apparently in commemoration of the idea that the Jews had caused the Black Death by poisoning its water. The well remained here until 1599.

16. *Getreidegasse ("Grain Street")*: This thoroughfare runs through the middle of the Old City and has always been a major commercial street. Jews have had businesses here pretty much whenever they were allowed to live in Salzburg, but especially in the early 20th century. When Adolf Hitler came to Salzburg in April 1938, shortly after the Annexation, he was greeted on *Getreidegasse* with enormous enthusiasm. The street was decked out with Nazi flags, and the uniforms of his SA Storm Troopers were much in evidence.

17. *Getreidegasse 9—Mozart's Birthplace*: Wolfgang Amadeus Mozart was born here in 1756, during the centuries when Jews were prohibited from spending more than an hour in the city of Salzburg. It is unlikely that he ever saw a real Jew in Salzburg, but he could not have missed seeing the Jews depicted on the "Jews' Sow" just up the street. His first interaction with live Jews took place when he went on tour as a child prodigy in 1764 and his father took him to London. An Italian born Jewish cellist named Emanuel Siprutini organized a concert for him there, and his father's diary noted encounters with four other Jews during that stay in London, both musicians and patrons. So Mozart may have learned some of his lack of prejudice against Jews from his father. As a young man Mozart bought a copy of Moses Mendlesohn's *Phädon, or the Immortality of the Soul*, and he seems to have drawn upon some of its themes when he wrote to tell his father about the death of his mother in Paris in 1778.

After Mozart moved to Vienna in 1781 to escape the musical conservatism of the "enlightened" Archbishop Colloredo, he collaborated with the Jewish born Lorenzo Da Ponte, who became the librettist for three of his finest operas, and possibly other works as well. Many anti-Jewish Viennese made a point of Da Ponte's Jewish background, but Mozart never mentioned it. He did mention the Jewish background of Baron Raimund Wetzler, referring to him first as "the rich converted Jew," then as "a rich Jew," and finally as "an honest friend." Indeed he was such a good friend that Mozart named his son Raimund after him, and Baron Wetzler served as Raimund Mozart's godfather during the young Mozart's short life. Even though Baron Raimund was a Catholic, Antisemites at the time rarely gave much credence to conversion, considering people like Da Ponte and Wetzler still to be Jews.

The only unconverted Jew Mozart is likely to have associated with in Vienna was Adam Isaac Arensteiner, Mozart's Orthodox neighbor and landlord for a year. Mozart wrote the *Abduction from the Seraglio* in Arensteiner's house. In the 1930s Nazi ideologues tried to claim Mozart as an Antisemite, focusing on two short quotes taken out of context. Like other Enlightenment Christians of his time Mozart may have retained some negative cultural stereotypes about Jews, but as a liberal Freemason he was an active promoter of tolerance and equality for Jews and was clearly not an Antisemite.

18. *Getreidegasse 14:* This was the site of Fleischmann and Company, before it was "Aryanized" in 1938 and turned over to Klara Müller.

19. *Getreidegasse 21:* This was Fuchs and Company, a fashions accessory store, owned by Isidor Fuchs and his brother-in-law Manfried Bonyhadi until 1938. Before moving to to this location on *Gerteidegasse* (sometime after 1926), the business had been on the other side of the river at *Mirabellplatz* 6. In an attempt to save their property from the 1938 "Aryaization" process, the owners turned it over to a loyal, non-Jewish employee named Franz Lipp. The Fuchs and Bonyhadi families then escaped to America before the war began, and their sons fought in the US Army.

Noncommissioned officer Isidor Fuchs, 1915.

When the young Sergeant Ernest Bonyhadi came back to Salzburg in 1945, Franz Lipp told him that he had preserved the business for his father and Mr. Fuchs. Ernest told this to his father, but Manfred Bonyhadi responded that Lipp had risked his life to help them and deserved to keep the property. The Fuchs and Bonyhadi families kept in touch with Franz Lipp after the war and sent him care packages of sugar and coffee during the shortages of 1946 and 1947. Lipp later moved the business down the street to *Getreidegasse* 46.

US Army Sergeant Ernest Bonyhadi in Salzburg, 1945.

20. Getreidegasse 24: Ornstein's Clothing Store was moved here in 1914. Ludwig Ornstein, originally "Luser" Ornstein, was a Jewish migrant from Austrian Poland. In 1897 he had opened a much smaller business at *Universitätsplatz* 3 (see §25). About 1904 he moved the shop for a few years to *Universitätsplatz* 9, where he shared quarters with a Rudolf Kohn. Later on he moved the business to *Getreidegasse* 13, and then, with the help of his half-brother Isaak (later "Jack") Neuwirth, he brought it to this location. Isaak, after volunteering for a stint with the Austrian Army and receiving a medal for his service in WWI, became a full partner with Ludwig.

Ludwig had two sons, Rudolf and Richard. Rudolf actively opposed Antisemitism in Austria, and was arrested in the 1920s for taking down Nazi placards. In 1926 he became the founding leader of the Salzburg Zionist Association. With the death of Ludwig and his wife in 1927 and 1928, Isaak continued to run the business with couple's two sons. In 1932 it was remodeled into a major department store. In the spring of 1938 Rudolf and Issak were arrested and sent to the prison camp at *Dachau*. Richard, however, had already settled in Palestine. The department store was then "Aryanized," being taken over by Kurt Thalhammer, a Nazi party activist who had joined the party in 1933.

Kurt Thalhammer's ad in 1938 announcing his takeover and transformation of Ornstein's Clothing Store into an "Aryan business."

After the War, Thalhammer was arrested and imprisoned for fifteen months for lying about his Nazi activities, and the American occupation forces put master tailor and concentration camp survivor Walter Fuchs in charge of the store. By then the Ornsteins had already escaped to the US, while the Neuwirths had been split up in their flight, some ending up in England, others making their way to America. Since neither family had a desire to return to Salzburg, they made Fuchs their manager. He managed the store until he retired in 1962, at which time it was sold to the *Modehaus Mühlberger* (Mühlberg House of Fashion).

Ornsteins' Clothing Store on Getreidegasse *in the 1930s. The hanging sign in front is still there today, but with a new name.*

21. Getreidegasse 26: This site has a long history as a brewery, a guesthouse and an inn. From the early 1600s to the mid 19th century it was called the Golden Lion and featured a large sign with a gilded lion over the entrance. By the 1890s the gilded lion was gone and the inn was called the *Schiesslerhaus*. A rented room here was used as the last temporary Jewish place of prayer before the construction of the *Lasserstrasse* Synagogue at the beginning of the 20th century.

A few years later this popular beer hall and meeting place was called *Mödlhammers*, and it continued to provide meeting rooms to all sorts of organizations. On August 24, 1921 a meeting was called here to form a Salzburg branch of the "German-Austrian Protection Society and Antisemitic League." The meeting was well attended, and 446 members signed up to found the Salzburg branch of the League. In 1982 it was turned into a McDonalds.

22. Getreidegasse 27: This house was owned by Jews in 1429 and may have remained in Jewish hands until the expulsion of 1498.

23. Getreidegasse 34 — *The Sternbräu Brewery Restaurant*: In the late 19th century this was the address of the *Sternbräu* ("Star Brew"), a brewery that had been operating here under one name or another since 1542. Salzburg's Jews rented a room here in the 1880s to set up the first Jewish place of prayer in Salzburg since the 15th century. Although the brewing operation moved to the other side of town in 1900, and the main entrance to the *Sternbräu* was moved to the *Griesgasse* side of the complex in 1926, the *Sternbräu* was still accessable from *Getreidegasse* in the 1930s.

Just to the right of the *Sternbräu* entrance was the antique shop of Bela and Therese Spiegel, who lived across the river at *Farberstrasse* 11. The antique shop was looted in the November 1938 "Crystal Night" (*Kristallnacht*) pogrom (see §67).

The Sternbräu *entrance (far left). The sign for Bela and Theresa Spiegel's Antique Shop is visible below the two stars advertising Star Beer, just behind the sign reading "GEH." Even though these are six-pointed stars, the* Sternbräu *was never Jewish.*

---

24. Universitätsplatz 9: From the 1880s through the first decade of the 20th century this was the location of Rudolf Kohn's clothing shop.

25. Universitätsplatz 3: This was the original location of Luser (Ludwig) Ornstein's clothing store (see §20).

26. *Festival Buildings (Festspiel Häuser) and Max Reinhardtplatz:* The young Jewish actor Max Reinhardt was born Max "Goldmann," but later adopted the non-Jewish name Reinhardt. He was very taken with the city when he worked in the Salzburg City Theater (*Stadttheater*) in 1893-94. After he became a famous theater director in Berlin and Vienna he had the idea to organize a "German national" cultural festival here. He envisioned it as something like the Wagner festival in Bayreuth, but broader in scope, encompassing theater, opera, music, and the arts.

As a small tourist city in the midst of a spectacular mountain setting, Salzburg seemed ideal for such a project. Reinhardt joined with Hugo von Hofmannsthal (a Catholic who had some Jewish ancestry), and the composer and conductor Richard Strauss in an attempt to organize the Salzburg Festival in 1917, but the midst of the First World War was not a good time to try to start such a project. Reinhardt was not easily discouraged, though, and liked Salzburg so much that he bought a home here the next year.

In 1920 Reinhardt and his associates succeeded in bringing off the first part of the project they had attempted in 1917. The square in front of the Cathedral was turned into an open-air theater and Reinhardt staged Hugo van Hofmannsthal's updated Catholic mystery play there (see §34). It was called *Jedermann* ("Everyman: A Play about the Death of a Rich Man"). The famous actor Alexander Moissi, who was widely believed to have been Jewish (see §43), and Reinhard's then paramour (later wife) Helene Thimig played the lead roles and the Festival was launched to worldwide acclaim.

In these days of numerous festivals of all sorts it is hard to imagine the impact of the Salzburg festival in the 1920s when it had no rivals. The Salzburg festival was like the Spoletto, the Aspen, and the Tanglewood music festivals all rolled into one—with the Cannes, Venice, and Berlin film festivals thrown in. While many of the leaders and performers were Jewish, the festival was a celebration of German, especially *Austrian* German, culture: Mozart, Beethoven, Goethe, and Schiller. At the time Stefan Zweig noted:

> The small city Salzburg with its 40,000 inhabitants that I had happily chosen for its romantic remoteness had transformed itself astonishingly. In the summer it had become the artistic and cultural capital, not only of Europe, but the entire world… All at once the Salzburg Festival had become a world attraction, a modern Olympic display of art where all nations competed to display their best performances. Nobody wanted to miss these exceptional presentations. Kings and princes, American millionaires and film stars, the friends of music, the artists, the poets and the snobs all

gathered in Salzburg in recent years; never had such a concentration of theatrical and musical achievement been successfully brought off in Europe as in this small city of small and long despised Austria... Salzburg was and remained in this decade the artistic pilgrimage center of Europe.[1]

After a few years of such success, the Festival was able to add the renovated winter riding school as a Festival Playhouse (*Festspielhaus*) to the plaza and churches where it was holding its performances. While the greater world flocked to the festival, ordinary Salzburgers often resented the displays of superior culture and wealth—especially in the hungry years of the early 1920s, and especially when flaunted by Jews. Max Reinhardt, Alexander Moissi, and the "Jewified" (*verjudet*) Festival were leading targets for Salzburg Antisemites in the 1920s. In 1922 von Hofmannsthal said: "these philistines will never choose Reinhardt for president [of the Festival]; they hate him—they hate him three- and four-fold: as a Jew, as the lord of a palace [he owned *Schloss Leopoldskron*], as an artist, and as a unique person beyond their comprehension."[2] Von Hoffmannsthal could have added another ground for their hatred, namely, Reinhardt's liaison with and later marriage to the beautiful Helene Thimig.

After the Nazis took power in Germany in 1933, the Festival became an exceptionally important place for German Jewish and anti-Nazi performers who were banned from Germany; but as Zweig noted, the pressure was rising in Salzburg too. Soon after Zweig fled Austria in 1934, Reinhardt moved to the more cosmopolitan New York City, returning only for the Festival seasons between 1935 and 1937. Then, when the Nazis took over Austria in 1938, they immediately "Aryanized" the Festival. They even removed some marble masks from the façade because of their "damned Jewish grins."

Festival Theater masks with "damned Jewish grins."

When Hitler arrived, he gave speeches in the Festival Theater, and a Führer Lodge was build for him in a second, Nazi renovated festival theater. In September 1938 the notorious "Degenerate Art Exhibition" (*entartete Kunstaustellung*) of modern art, which was deemed immoral by the Nazis, opened in the Festival Theater and drew 40,000 visitors. Max Reinhardt's home in *Schloss Leopoldskron* was "Aryanized," as was the *Salzkammergut* home of Hugo von Hofmannsthal's widow after she was stripped of her German citizenship in 1943.

SS Chief Heinrich Himmler at the Festival Theater in March 1939, flanked on his right by SS Holocaust organizers Ernst Kaltenbrunner and Arthur Seyss-Inquart.

Despite the importation of Wilhelm Furtwängler from the Berlin Philharmonic and the renovation of the Festival Playhouse, the Salzburg Festival lost its international appeal and degenerated into just another Nazi gala. But when WWII ended, the surviving stalwarts of the old festival rallied around to revive it. In 1946 exiles like Helene Thimig-Reinhardt, Elisabeth Schumann, Emanuel List, Fritz Busch, and Bruno Walter (who had earlier been removed as director of the Vienna State Opera and the Salzburg Festival), among many others, organized an "American Friends of the Salzburg Festival." Holding a benefit concert for the Festival in New York's Metropolitan Opera House in 1947, they soon returned to perform at the Festival, joined by Jewish artists like Jehudi Menuhin and Jewish-born converts to Christianity like Otto Klemperer (who had been treated as Jewish under the Nazis' Nuremberg Racial Laws). Eventually the Festival was restored to some of its pre-war glory as a center for world culture. In 1960 the Festival Playhouse became the "Little Festival Playhouse," when the new, Large Festival Playhouse opened next door.

In the postwar years the Festival Playhouse also staged events that were conspicuously not related to high culture. In December 1947 it hosted a boxing match between the Salzburg Athletic Club (*ATSV*) and Jewish boxers sponsored by the Linz section of the Austrian Jewish Athletic League (the *Hakoa*). Some Salzburgers shouted Antisemitic comments at the Jewish boxers and Jewish fans responded vigorously. Soon the confrontation escalated into a general brawl, from which the Jewish contingent emerged victorious. This was the last boxing match at the Festival Playhouse—something music lovers did not regret.

Hitler in the Festival Theater.

27. Toscanini Court: This courtyard, adjacent to the Festival Playhouse, is named after the famous, longtime conductor of the Salzburg Festsival Orchestra, Arturo Toscanini. A prominent opponent of Fascism, Toscanini notified the Festival authorities in 1938 that, in light of the changed conditions, he was no longer willing to work with the *Festspiel*.

28. Furtwängler Garden: Behind *Max Reinhardt Platz* is a garden named after the famous orchestra leader Wilhelm Furtwängler. Director of the Berlin Philharmonic, Furtwängler did not share Toscanini's scruples. Becoming Nazi Germany's premier conductor and Hitler's favorite before the Annexation, he took over the Festival job in 1938 and entertained 5,000 participants in the Nazi "Strength through Joy" program. After WWII Furtwängler was banned from conducting in Austria for one year, but he returned to the Festival podium in the summer of 1948 and was the Festival's leading conductor for the next several years.

29. *Franciscan Steet and Cloister (Franziskanergasse and Franziskanerkloster)*: The Franciscan Cloister started as a convent in the 12th century, but was converted into a Franciscan monastery in 1583 as part of the Counter-Reformation campaign against Protestantism. The old City Parish Church (*Stadtpfarrkirche*) across the street had become a hotbed of Protestantism in the 16th century, and the Franciscans were brought in to restore it to Catholicism. The City Parish Church was renamed the Franciscan Church (*Franziskannerkirche*), and every resident of the city of Salzburg was required to take an oath of loyalty to the Pope or face expulsion from the Archbishopric.

In October 1938 the Nazis seized the Cloister for a *Gestapo* Headquarters, and Archbishop Waitz's protest against the expropriation led to some tense moments as the Nazis sought to silence him (see §33).

Clearing out the Fransiscan Cloister to make room for the Gestapo.

30. *St. Peter's Church and Peterskeller*: *Peterskeller* ("Peter's Cellar") is reputed to be the oldest inn in Central Europe because it is identified with the one reported to have been next to St. Peter's Church when Charlemagne came to Salzburg in the year 803. It seems, however, that the St. Peter's of 803 may have been located elsewhere. In any case, the current location has been the home of St. Peter's for a thousand years, and the monks of St. Peter's have had a wine cellar here for many centuries.

By the 19th century the rooms of *Peterskeller* had become a popular locale for the meetings of numerous organizations. On the evening of November 3, 1911, the Salzburg Rabbi Dr. Adolf Altman presented a lecture on the history of Jews in Salzburg here before the Society for Salzburg Regional Studies (*Salzburger Landeskunde*). In 1988 *Dr. Adolf Altmann-Strasse* was dedicated to his memory (see §48).

That Dr. Altmann, then in the process of preparing his magisterial *History of the Jews in the City and Province of Salzburg*, was invited to present a lecture to this elite gathering was a sign of the acceptance Jews had gained from some segments of Salzburg society. Indeed, he was inducted as a member of the Society, which already included, among others: Archbishop Katschthaler, Liberal Party leader Julius Haagn, and attorney Julius Sylvester—who had been the leading German Nationalist promoter of "modern" Antisemitism in late 19th century Salzburg.

Rabbi Altmann in 1913.

Yet other segments of Salzburg society were not so accepting. The Catholic, clerical, and Antisemitic *Salzburg Chronicle* (*Salzburger Chronik*) wondered that a Rabbi was "permitted" to address such a gathering. The *Chronicle* report denounced Altmann's talk for an alleged "lack of objectivity" and said that the topic would have been better addressed by a "more serious" researcher who would focus on the poverty of Christians in the Middle Ages caused by "hard-hearted, dirty Jewish usurers." The *Chronicle* concluded with a warning that the Jews were still seeking revenge against the Salzburgers because their predecessors had expelled them.

A few years later, in 1914, this same Christian-Social Party affiliated *Chronicle* made it clear that there was no distinction between racial Antisemitism and old fashioned Christian Jew-hatred. The article in question concluded that "in Austria every upstanding person is an Antisemite." The *Chronicle* and most of the other Salzburg papers were already so Antisemitic that the *Iron Broom* was hard pressed to stand out in the 1920s (though still managed to do so). The Christian-Social Party, the political party of the Catholics, was as Antisemitic as the *Chronicle*. The 1918 and 1926 programs of the Christian-Social Party called for the "sharpest defensive warfare against the Jewish danger," and promised that the party would fight against "the demoralizing Jewish influence in spiritual and economic realms." After the Nazi period, the Christian-Social Party was rebuilt as the conservative Austrian People's Party. The revived party has, for the most part, rejected its Antisemitic heritage, but some of its leaders did engage in Antisemitic rhetoric during the Waldheim affair in the 1980s and in a 2006 dispute over restoring some art works stolen by the Nazis to their rightful owners.

Antisemitic election poster from 1920 showing a "Jewish" snake strangling an Austrian Eagle. The words read: "Vote Christian-Social! German Christians Save Austria."

31. *St. Petersbezirk 5:* The Antisemitic League and the *Iron Broom* set up their headquarters here after leaving *Judengasse* (see §8).

32. *Kapitelplatz:* In November 1938 the Nazis built a memorial here to the Nazi militants who died in the failed attempts to seize power in Munich in 1923 and Austria in 1934. It was later the site of an impressive Nazi funeral for General Eugen Beyer, one of the few high ranking German Army officers who had come out of the Austrian Army.

33. *The Cathedral (Dom):* The Cathedral was the spiritual center of the Catholic Church in Catholic-ruled Salzburg. After several earlier cathedrals were destroyed by fire, the Konrad Cathedral was built here in 1181, lasting until it too burned down in 1598. The original version of the current cathedral was built in the 1620s, and was restored after severe damage from the 1944 American bombing of Salzburg. Late in WWII the American air force began a heavy bombardment of Salzburg and the Cathedral was hit.

Hatred of Jews waxed and waned in the Catholic Church of Salzburg over the centuries. When a political Antisemitism, aligned with German Nationalism, was on the rise in Austria during the 1880s, it was complemented by Antisemitic literature from the Vatican. It is all the more striking, therefore, that Dr. Josef Anton Schöpf, a Catholic priest, theology professor, Salzburg Episcopal Counselor, and protégée of Archbishop Friedrich von Schwarzenberg, took up the struggle against it. In the last decades of the 19th century he published a series of pamphlets opposing Antisemitism in all its forms. In one of these he told a story about Emanuell Veith, the Salzburg Cathedral Cannon. Schöpf wrote that Veith, "a born Jew, declared from the Cathedral pulpit that the maliciously spread lie that Jews need the blood of a Christian child to celebrate their Easter holiday [Passover] is a spiteful, blasphemous libel, and neither the Old Testament nor the writings of the *Talmud*...contained anything of the sort." A later Salzburg priest and theology professor named Alois Mager followed in the footsteps of Dr. Schöpf. Campaigning against the Antisemitic measures of the Nazis, he was arrested by the *Gestapo*.

By contrast, Sigmund Waitz, the Archbishop who headed the Salzburg church when the Nazis took over Austria, told a meeting of Catholic academics in 1925, "the Jews have became a worldwide menace." But once the Nazis were in charge, Waitz might have had second thoughts about who was the worldwide menace. After he protested against the Nazi seizure of several church properties, the Nazis mounted a demonstration in front of his residence. Three thousand Nazi activists and Hitler Youth whistled and cried: "We want to see our Archbishop—in *Dachau*."

By then Waitz was too busy defending the prerogatives of the Catholic Church to concern himself with what happened to Salzburg's Jews, and he criticized foreigners who concerned themselves with the persecution of Jews rather than the travails of the Church. The

Nazis' conflict with the Catholic Church died down when the Nazis saw that it could interfere with their war effort, but only because they had decided to postpone their campaign to subordinate the Catholic Church until after they won the War.

Waitz' successor, Andreas Rohracher, was installed in 1943. He paid a holiday visit after the War to comfort his Catholic Nazi and SS parishioners held in the American prison in Salzburg, Camp Orr (see §42). He called their imprisonment brutal, though he and his predecessor had said nothing of the kind against the far more brutal *Dachau* and *Mauthausen* Concentration Camps with their branch camps, run in and near Salzburg by the Nazis. He had, however, been one of the first to denounce the Nazi "euthanasia" campaign in which gas chambers were first developed to kill handicapped Germans (mostly Christians).

Rohracher also campaigned for a Nazi amnesty in the late 1940s, saying it was time to heal the wounds of hatred and war. He had pity for former Nazis and their fellow travelers, even intervening personally to win the release of some major perpetrators. Like some of his predecessors he seems to have been virulently anti-Jewish, if not actually Antisemitic, during the 1930s and 1940s. He even delivered an Easter sermon in 1946 that blamed "the Jews" for the crucifixion, marshalling a fervor that would have impressed Christian Jew haters of earlier centuries. But if he did not change his mind, he at least saw the way the world had changed in the aftermath of the Second Vatican Council, when the Catholic Church officially rejected the claim that the Jews were responsible for killing Jesus. He attended the opening of the restored *Lasserstrasse* synagogue in 1968 in a gesture of good will that surprised many at the time.

In 1993, Archbishop Georg Eder took a major step beyond all his predecessors. He welcomed a volume of essays in honor of the 125th anniversary of the official Salzburg Jewish Community (*Israelitische Kultusgemeinde*) with these words:

> One cannot read the chronicle of the Jewish Community in Salzburg without deep emotion and shame. How much suffering had this small remnant of Israel to endure under us and also from us—from the first pogrom to the year

1938!... Many times the Jews were driven away from Salzburg, but they have always returned. It is well that they regard Salzburg as their homeland, and that despite bitter experiences they have never given it up. So in this manifold Jubilee Year, I salute the Salzburg Jewish Community as children and sons of Abraham, who is also for us Christians the "father of faith."[3]

34. *Cathedral Square* (*Domplatz*): The Salzburg Festival began when Max Reinhardt staged the first performance of Hugo van Hofmannsthal's "Everyman" (*Jedermann*) here in 1920 (see §26). Staging the play here became an annual event and was the core of the Festival before the Nazi years. It was also the subject of much comment by Nazis and some Antisemitic Catholics, who objected to the "Jew Festival" taking over this space in front of the Catholic Cathedral, thereby forcing good Catholics to go around the "Jewish pollution" to get to Mass. Naturally the Nazis put a stop to that when they took over in 1938. But on August 1, 1946, the Salzburg Festival resumed the performance of "Everyman" on the Cathedral Square, and it has been performed here every year since.

35. *Residence Square* (*Residenzplatz*): Shortly after they took control of Salzburg, local Nazis emulated their German counterparts by staging a public book-burning. Over twelve hundred banned books were thrown into the fire on the square in front of the Archbishop's Residence on April 30, 1938. These included the works of Salzburg's most famous Jewish author Stefan Zweig, and Festival author Hugo von Hofmannsthal. The Nazi-dominated Teachers' Union organized the event, and Salzburg teachers led their students in feeding the inferno. It was the only such book burning in Austria.

Book burning, April 30, 1938.

The books burned in Salzburg would have included those of the German Jewish poet Heinrich Heine, who had written prophetically: "Wherever they burn books, in the end they will burn people." On April 30, 2007 there was a public ceremony commemorating the 1938 book burning. It included readings from some of the burned books, and featured Robert Schindler and Vladimir Vertlieb, two of the most important Jewish authors in today's Austria, reading from their own works.

Robert Schindler reading from his work at the book burning memorial ceremony in 2007.

36. *Residenzplatz 1:* In 2004 the Unversity of Salzburg opened a new Center for Jewish Cultural History here in the Old Residence. Scholars from several different fields, including history, law, theology and linguistics, are now affiliated with this research center, directed by University Professor Dr. Gerhard Langer. The center is developing a research library for public use that will include a large number of interviews with Salzburg's Jewish Holocaust survivors, as well as numerous other resources. Anyone wanting to learn more about Salzburg's Jewish history would do well to start here. The center can be reached by telephone at +43 (0)662 8044-2962, and its web site can be found at: *www.sbg.ac.at/zjk*

37. *Mozart Square (Mozartplatz) — The New Residence (Neue Residenz):* This palace was built in 1588 as a temporary Residence and later guesthouse for Archbishop Wolf Dietrich. In 1918, Mozart Square was the entryway to the provincial government building when the Social Democrats assembled here during a hunger march.

Faced with a show of force, the crowd turned to looting, emptying the wine cellar in the *Peterskeller*, stealing the Persian carpets from the Hôtel de l'Europe, and looting everything from Schwarz's Department Store (see §10 and 120). From 1939 to 1945 the New Residence

1918 hunger demonstration in Mozart Square.

From the Mozartplatz go up Pfeifergasse to the entry to the Chiemseehof on the right.

38. Chiemseehof: The former palace of the Bishop of Chiemsee, this has been the site of the Salzburg provincial government (*Landesregierung*) since 1862. On August 7-8, 1920, the National Socialist Parties of all German speaking territories held a convention in Salzburg and met in the chambers of the provincial assembly. Among the participants was a then obscure Munich agitator named Adolf Hitler, who appeared in a group photo of the participants.

*Nazi Convention participants in 1920.
Adolf Hitler is in the fourth row, marked with a rectangle.*

Hitler's contribution to the discussions so impressed the party leaders that he was asked to address the public meeting in the Salzburg Spa (*Kurhaus*) that evening, thus speeding his rise to party leadership. When the Austrian Nazis returned to Salzburg for their 1923 convention, the Social Democrats tried to keep them out of the Chiemseehof facilities, but they were overruled by the other parties. By then Hitler had risen to the leadership of the Nazi movement, and so attended the convention as the Munich Party Leader, or Führer. This time the Chiemseehof was guarded by steel helmeted Nazi Stormtroopers.

Continue up the street to Kajetanerplatz and turn right onto Kaigasse; then, after a few yards, make a U-turn up Nonnbergstiege on the left, and go to the top of the stairs.

39. Nonnberg Lookout 1—Jews' Mountain (Judenberg): In the center of the view across the river from the top of the stairs is the mountain called the *Gaisberg*, each extension of which has a name. Just to the right of the rocky cliffs below the peak, is a slope with some large, open green areas that have buildings visible in them. The largest of the buildings is a hotel that was built on the *Judenberg Alm* ("Jews' Mountain Pasture") in the 1950s. This part of the *Gaisberg* is called the "Jews' Mountain" (*Judenberg*). There seems to be no record of how it got that name, but it was referred to as such at least as far back as 1442, so it is likely that there was some connection between that part of the mountain and Jews in the 15th century or earlier.

From 1889 to 1931 there was a cog railway running up the *Judenberg* for the wonderful views; and there was a chair lift in the 1950s. Hikers can still get those views by taking City Bus number six to the end of the line in *Parsch*, walking up to the end of *Gaisbergstrasse*, and then up to the end of *Judenbergweg*. Follow the small trail along the stream and keep going in that direction, ignoring the gravel roads it crosses. About half an hour up the trail is the fantastic view from just in front of the Hotel *Kobenzl*, 1,200 feet above the city. You will see Salzburg and its castle down below, the Salzach River Valley going off to the southern mountains, and the German valley leading to *Berchtesgaden*, with the sharp peak of the nearly 9,000 ft. tall *Gross Watzmann* straight ahead, framed between the two closer mountains, the *Untersberg* and *Hoher Göll*.

From this height on a clear day you can also see both the site of Hitler's mountain retreat, on the slope of the *Kehlstein* branch of *Hoher Göll*, and that of his so-called "Eagle's Nest," built high up on the *Kehlstein* peak to impress foreign guests. Hitler rarely went there himself as he was afraid of heights.

Serious hikers can proceed up the next stretch for another twenty minutes to the *Zistelalm*, 650 feet higher up, for some even more spectacular views. Or they can go on for about an hour to the very top of *Gaisberg*. Non-hikers, or those who prefer to hike only downhill, can get to *Kobenzl*, *Zistelalm*, and the *Gaisberg* by taking City Bus number 151 (marked *Gaisberg*) that leaves from the *Mirabell Platz* bus stop.

Proceed through the gate ahead and go around to the Nonnberg Kirche.

40. Nonnberg Cloister and Church: This famous cloister was founded around 700 CE as the first women's cloister north of the Alps. The church building dates back to the year 1,000 CE, though it burned and was rebuilt in the 15th century. In 1498 a gold plated, silver box used to store consecrated wafers (the Host) was reported missing from the church. Given the events of 1404 (see §6 and 27), it was suspected that Jews had stolen it to desecrate the Host it contained. The new Archbishop Leonhard von Keutschach had come from *Carinthia*, where all the Jews had been expelled in 1496, along with Jews from all the other Habsburg territories. He had resisted expelling the Jews from Salzburg in 1496, in order to demonstrate his independence from both the Emperor in Vienna and the city leaders of Salzburg, who were urging him to follow suit.

But with the *Nonnberg* Church accusations, Leonhard decided to act before his authority was usurped by a Salzburg mob. Striving to retain his authority, and giving in to his own prejudices against Jews, he issued a declaration of expulsion from all the territories under his rule. He claimed to be acting of his own free will and denied that he was giving in to mass pressure, or that the *Nonnberg* Church theft had anything to do with his decision. Instead, he said it was to "protect" his Christian subjects from the burden the Jews allegedly imposed on the poor. Under this order Jews were still allowed to pass through the Archbishopric on their travels, but they now had to pay a special tax and were forbidden from spending more than one hour in the city.

Before being expelled, the Jews from Salzburg and other towns under Archbishop Leonhard's rule were required to sign a promise never to return, and Leonhard ordered the synagogues "cleansed" — two measures that prefigured Nazi tactics and terminology. Leonhard's tax on Jewish travelers remained in effect until Archbishop Colloredo cancelled it in 1791. That was six years after Colloredo had ordered the "Jews' Sow" on the Town Hall destroyed, and five years after he had demonstrated his open-mindedness by visiting a synagogue during a trip to Amsterdam. Colloredo repealed the tax and even allowed Jewish merchants to remain in the vicinity overnight as long as they stayed outside the city limits. Even so, he directed the police to maintain a close watch over all Jews while they were in his territories.

After leaving the Church go to the railing across the way and to the left of the main entrance.

41. Nonnberg Lookout 2—a) Hallein: From this Lookout in front of *Nonnberg* Church there is a magnificent view of southern Salzburg and the mountains in the distance. A conspicuous smokestack, usually with a long white plume, appears to the left of the wooded hill that houses *Schloss Hellbrunn*, marking the town of *Hallein*, 15 km to the south. Through most of the Middle Ages, as in pre-Roman times, *Hallein* with its salt mines was a more important trade center than Salzburg. It also had a larger and more important Jewish community than Salzburg until the Jews of *Hallein* were wiped out in the Black Death massacres of 1349. As with the town of Salzburg, Archbishop Pilgrim's encouragement of foreign traders led to the reestablishment of a Jewish community in Hallein later in the 14th century. But in 1404 its members shared the same fate as the Salzburg Jews, and were burned to death. The *Hallein* Jewish community was reestablished in the 15th century and survived until the remaining handful of Jews living there were expelled by Archbishop Leonhard's order in 1498.

In the early 1940s the *Waffen* SS set up a barracks for 1500-2000 men near *Hallein*, and in 1943 they opened a new branch of the *Dachau* concentration camp which held up to ninety prisoners, in a nearby stone quarry. Prisoners there were worked until exhausted and then shot.

In 1946 a camp for DPs, or "Displaced Persons" (the post-war term for refugees and death camp survivors) was set up in *Hallein-Puch*. This was a town just north of *Hallein* proper, a mile or two closer to Salzburg. This camp for Jewish refugees operated into the 1950s. According to the camp council's stamp it was called "House of Israel" (*Bejt Israel*). There is a story that during the food shortages of 1946 the local people were outraged to find that Jews from the camp had thrown pork sausages into the trash, and the incident became the subject of a great deal of Antisemitic comment.

Orthodox Jews in the Hallein-Puch DP Camp.

42. *Nonnberg Lookout 2— b) Lager Glasenbach:* Looking closer and to the left, at the southern edge of the city where *Alpenstrasse* comes closest to the *Salzach* River, there is a bridge over to the village of *Glasenbach*. The district north of the bridge on this side of the river is now called the Alpine Settlement (*Alpensiedlung*). In 1945 the American occupation forces set up an internment camp for captured SS troops and Nazi Party members there. They named it Camp Marcus W. Orr, but because the soldiers guarding the camp were housed in the *Glasenbach* barracks across the river, Camp Orr became known as Camp *Glasenbach* (*Lager Glasenbach*). For Jewish soldiers assigned to *Glasenbach*, like Bernard Robinson, the task of guarding SS troops who had massacred Jews was particularly difficult. He never forgot the answer a young SS man gave him when asked how he could have killed Jewish children: the SS man said earnestly that he had to do it, otherwise the children would have grown up. Robinson managed to get reassigned to help a Jewish chaplain working with DPs.

Camp Marcus W. Orr, from the outside, 1946.

In January of 1947 the Salzburg Archbishop, Andreas Rohracher, visited *Glasenbach* to comfort these members of his flock, and in March he denounced the "harshness" of the anti-Nazi laws, calling for the prisoners' release. De-Nazification had turned into a bureaucratic mess in Austria, where 600,000 party members constituted a large part of the adult population. Major perpetrators often had the connections to get excused, since prominent figures like Archbishop Rohracher were willing to intervene on their behalf, although minor figures and even fellow travelers were caught by the system. After a short period in which a few major perpetrators were targeted for prosecution and forty-three were sentenced to death, the vast majority of the Nazi and SS prisoners were released without any attempt to hold individuals responsible for their war crimes.

Camp Marcus W. Orr, interior, 1946 (with castle in background, left).

In the summer of 1947 Camp *Glasenbach* was closed down. Dr. Hubert Hueber, Salzburg *Gestapo* chief since 1942, was held there until it closed, and was then transferred to a regular prison for a while longer. His brutal subordinate, *Gestapo* officer Georg König, was also interned in *Glasenbach* until it closed, at which time he was mistakenly released and escaped to Germany. When he was finally caught in 1957, he was sentenced to two more years in prison (making for a total of only four years). An amnesty was instituted in June 1948 for all but the chief offenders.

43. Nonnberg Lookout 2— c) Alexander Moissi Straße: Across *Alpenstraße*, and a short block to the west of the former Camp *Glasenbach*, is a short street named after the famous "Albanian Jewish" actor Alexander Moissi. He was born in Austrian Trieste in 1879 to Albanian parents who are widely believed to have been Jewish (though some researchers dispute that). He spent most of his first ten years in Albania before returning to Trieste. He first appeared on the stage of the Vienna City Theater (*Burgtheater*) in 1898, and later rose to stardom in Berlin, where he became a close associate of Max Reinhardt.

He was particularly famous for his deeply psychological portrayal of dramatic figures from Shakespeare, Ibsen, and Tolstoi, and made his cinema debut in 1913 in "Dark Fate" (*Das schwarze Los*). He is often referred to as the greatest German-speaking actor of the inter-war period. In 1920, Moissi was the first to play the title role in "Everyman" (*Jedermann*) at the Salzburg Festival. Like Reinhardt, Moissi was subjected to many attacks from Salzburg Antisemites, but he continued to perform "Everyman" in Salzburg every year until 1934. With his German career finished and his Austrian prospects looking dim, he applied for Italian citizenship, but he died of pneumonia in 1935 before he was able to complete the process. There is also a *Moissistraße* named for him in Berlin.

44. *Nonnberg Lookout 2 — d) Jewish Cemetery, Uferstrasse 47:*
Across the river from Camp *Glasenbach*, and a little to the north (left), is the Jewish cemetery (just south of the intersection between *Uferstrasse* and *Valkenauerstrasse*). A *Chewra-Kadischa* burial society was founded in 1893 and bought this land for a cemetery in what was then the independent village of *Aigen*. The *Aigen* district officials objected to the cemetery, saying it was offensive to the religion of *Aigen's* Catholic residents, but the provincial authorities rejected their protest. Rudolf Fürst, who had died the previous December, was the first to be buried here, after his body was exhumed and transferred from the municipal cemetery.

A curiosity is the burial of Leon Zucker in 1898. He had died suddenly in the railroad station while traveling through Salzburg and, taken to be a Jew from his name and appearance, was buried in the Jewish cemetery. When his effects were examined later, it was discovered that he was a Christian convert and an English missionary, but his grave was left undisturbed until the Nazis took over.

As the community aged, the cemetery filled slowly at a rate of one or two burials a year until a flood of desperate refugees from the east poured into camps near Salzburg during WWI. As a result, fifteen Jews were buried here in 1917, eight more in 1918, and four more in 1919. Then the burial rate dropped back to its pre-war level. In 1938 the Nazis seized the property. After deciding it had "no anthropological value," they sold it to Maria Frenkenberger, the former caretaker. She sold 68 of the 100 gravestones and turned the mortuary into a barn for animals that she pastured in the cemetery.

In August 1945 American occupation forces took control of the property and annulled the sale to Frenkenberger. Judging by an Army report, the American investigators were shocked by the desecration of the cemetery and the filth that covered the graves. They soon transferred ownership of the cemetery to the reestablished Jewish community and it has been restored with loving care. Yet shortly after its transfer in 1947, a street leading to the cemetery was renamed *Valkenauerstrasse* after the 15th century sculptor who carved the "Jews' Sow" for the Salzburg Town Hall. In 2008 a municipal committee was established to consider renaming some streets with Nazi or Antisemitic associations, and *Valkenauerstrasse* was one of those taken under consideration.

The city of Salzburg has now added an attractive memorial apologizing for the vandalization of the cemetery in the Nazi years and listing the names and dates of all those buried here before 1939 whose gravestones were destroyed. Indeed, in recent years the cemetery has become the site of an impressive military ceremony in November, on Austrian Memorial Day, to commemorate the Jews who fought and died for Austria before the Nazi take over, and to remember those who were persecuted and murdered between 1938 and 1945.

A military salute before the commemorative plaques (in background) during the Austrian Memorial Day ceremony.

The cemetery is open for viewing, but visitors need to contact the synagogue office via email < office@ikg-salzburg.at > or call 662-87-2288 prior to coming, as there is no longer a resident caretaker and the gate is locked to prevent vandalism.

45. Nonnberg Lookout 2— e) Camp Hellbrunn: Just below *Nonnberg*, to the left (southeast), behind a sports field and between the open fields of the *Nonntal* district and the *Salzach* River, are an old retirement home, the Salzburg State archives, and the Natural Sciences faculty of the University of Salzburg. The retirement home and its general vicinity were originally an Austrian army barracks and its parade grounds. After having been used by the German Army during WWII, this became the second largest camp for DPs in Salzburg. It was named "Camp *Hellbrunn*" because it was on the road to *Hellbrunn* Palace (*Schloss Hellbrunn*). Salzburgers, however, called it the "Polish Camp," because half its residents came from Poland.

At the end of 1945, after many non-Jewish refugees had returned to their homes, the camp had two to three thousand residents, including 500 children. As long as the occupation authorities ran the camp it had a kosher kitchen. But when the Austrians took over the camp administration, they closed the kitchen, saying it was a "medically unnecessary special diet" that met only private concerns and was therefore undeserving of government funding.

By the 1950s most of the Jewish DPs were gone, and Camp *Hellbrunn* served mostly ethnic German refugees (*Volksdeutsche*) who had been expelled from Czechoslovakia and Hungary. The present retirement home was created for elderly and invalid DPs, and was renovated by the United Nations' High Commission for Refugees in 1956-58 before it was transformed into a municipal home for the aged in 1961.

46. Nonnberg Lookout 2— f) Mascagnigasse: Between the former site of Camp *Helbrunn* and *Alpenstraße* is a small residential street called *Mascagnigasse*. Vladamir Vertlib, the most famous Jewish writer to live in Salzburg since Stefan Zweig left in 1934, has his home on this street. Vertlib was born in Leningrad Russia in 1966, but emigrated as a child in 1971 with his family. They lived in Israel, Austria, Israel again, and the USA, before finally settling in Austria in 1981. His first book, *The Deportation* (*Die Abschiebung*), was published in 1995 and gave his readers a beautifully written and insightful view of this childhood odyssey. Since then he has published a number of books and other works that deal with themes relating to being Jewish in present-day Austria.

Vladimir Vertleib reading from his work, The Deportation.

This tour of the Old City (= Part I) can be ended here. For those who choose to continue: go back around Nonnberggasse, *and go up the hill past the Castle entrance (possibly stopping on the way for refreshment at the Stiegl beer-garden, which has lovely views of the old city and very good beer). After the steep climb up to the Castle, continue out* O. Kokoschka Weg *to the* Richter Höhe *("Richter Heights"), on the southwest corner of the* Mönchsberg.

47. Richter Höhe Lookout—a) Schloss Leopoldskron: Clearly visible below are the lake and the *Schloss Leopoldskron* ("Leopold's Crown Palace"). This lovely palace was built for Archbishop Leopold Anton Freiherr von Firmian in the 1740s. Leopold had no Jews in his territories, but he persecuted, expropriated, and expelled some 20,000

Protestants from the Archbishopric during his rule, including a large group of Salzburgers who later settled in the British North American colony of Georgia.

In the 1850s *Schloss Leopoldskron* was the summer home of the deposed King Ludwig I of Bavaria, who had been forced to abdicate in 1848 after a notorious liaison with a dancer who called herself Lola Montez. The Palace suffered from great neglect in the later 19th and early 20th centuries until the famous Jewish theater director Max Reinhardt bought it in 1918. Reinhardt went on to found the Salzburg festival, and the restored palace became a major social center for the international art scene that came to Salzburg every summer (see §26).

Then came the German "Annexation" of Austria, and *Schloss Leopoldskron* was "Aryanized." Some Antisemites could not bear to refer to Reinhardt as a "theater director"—that was far too respectful. Instead, in their newspapers and official documents they often used his 1921 purchase of some inns around the lake to call him an "innkeeper." As was common when the Nazis seized desirable properties, there was a struggle over the loot. In this case, local Nazis, and even the powerful Regional Governor (*Gauleiter*) Friedrich Rainer, were pushed aside as Hitler himself designated *Schloss Leopoldskron* as a guesthouse for prominent artists visiting the festival plays.

After the war, the American occupation authorities returned the Palace to Max Reinhardt's heirs (he had died in New York City in 1943), but as his heirs had no interest in returning to live in Salzburg, they made *Schloss Leopoldskron* available for other purposes. In 1947 the first Salzburg Seminar in American Studies was held here, sponsored by Harvard University. In 1950 the Palace was put up for sale and bought by a foundation dedicated to maintaining the Salzburg Seminars, which it still does today.

48. *Richter Höhe Lookout—b) Dr. Adolf Altmann Strasse:* Past the end of the *Leopoldskron* Lake and slightly to the left you can see the municipal cemetery. Right in front of the cemetery, and cutting across a curve in *Berchtesgadner Strasse*, is the stretch of the old *Berchtesgadner*

Road that has been named after Rabbi Altmann. In addition to his two-volume history of Salzburg's Jews and his long service as Rabbi in Salzburg, Adolf Altmann was a field rabbi in the Austrian Army during WWI and was awarded a Gold Cross for bravery in the face of the enemy.

Rabbi Altmann with his Salzburg students

Rabbi Altmann in uniform 1916.

In 1920 Rabbi Altmann went on to become the Chief Rabbi in Trier Germany, where he remained until he was forced to flee to Holland in 1938. The German invasion of the Netherlands in 1940 brought him back into the hands of the Nazis. After many tribulations he died in Auschwitz in May 1944 and his wife was killed in a gas chamber there in July. There is also a *Dr. Adof Altmann Strasse* in Trier.

Rabbi Altmann leading Jewish services for Jewish soldiers in the Dolomite mountains in 1917.

49. Richter Höhe Lookout—c) Gypsy Camp Leopoldskron-Maxglan: Far beyond the end of the *Leopoldskron* Lake and to the right, along the stream called the *Glanbach*, was the city of Salzburg's only concentration camp (technically an *Anhaltslager*/holding camp rather than a *Konzentationslager*/concentration camp, but there was little difference). Jews were not the only "racial" group slated for extermination by the Nazis. While a few high ranking Nazi Party racial theorists had argued that "pure" Gypsies were Aryans and should be preserved, the popular prejudice in Germany and Austria against Gypsies was probably stronger than that against Jews, and local officials throughout the *Reich* pressed for a "final solution" to the Gypsy "problem." (In the end, a higher proportion of Austria's Gypsies than Austria's Jews was killed. This, however, reflected their greater poverty, and the even greater reluctance of other countries to take in Gypsies, rather than any greater stringency on the part of the Nazis.)

Salzburg became the major center for rounding up Gypsies in western Austria. At first they were put in the horse stalls at the Salzburg racetrack (like the Japanese-Americans from Los Angeles, who were interned at the Santa Anita Racetrack in 1941). But when the prisoners grew too numerous for this temporary camp and plans to deport them to Poland were postponed, a secure concentration camp was built in the wetlands along the *Glanbach*. Most of the men were shipped out to slave labor camps, where they were put to work building the autobahns and channeling streams (something to remember while appreciating the fine highways of Austria and Germany), while the women and children were kept here.

In the fall of 1940 Adolf Hitler's favorite director Leni Riefenstahl made a movie called *Tiefland* ("Lowlands") that required some Gypsies for background roles. The SS provided her with thirty to forty real Gypsies from the Salzburg camp—mostly children—along with a few SS guards to keep them in line. For a few weeks they enjoyed the better conditions of the film production camp, before they were shipped back to *Leopoldskron-Maxglan*. Riefenstahl's film company paid the SS for the service, while the Gypsy extras remained unpaid.

Late in 1942 the Nazis ended their uncertainty as to whether Gypsies were really Aryans, and the order came to ship the inmates of the Salzburg *Leopoldskron-Maxglan* concentration camp to *Auschwitz-Birkenau*. Only a few of the inmates, including a handful of the children from *Tiefland*, survived the extermination camps. In 1985 Salzburg built a memorial on the *Ignaz-Rieder-Kai* (see §135), where the first Gypsy camp was located, for the three hundred Gypsies of the Salzburg camps.

The Gypsy Memorial on the Ignaz-Rieder-Kai.

After the war, Gypsy survivors fared even worse than their Jewish counterparts. They were often identified as "asocial" (that is "antisocial") inmates rather than as "racial" or "political" victims, and thus denied even the minimal benefits that went to other survivors. Sometimes they even suffered further persecution. On September 18, 1945, the police ordered a newly arrived encampment of sixty Gypsies to leave Salzburg immediately or face arrest.

Today there are still many Europeans who say that the Gypsies were criminals and not the victims of persecution. One Gypsy reported in 1986 that after fifteen years in Salzburg he was still harassed in his home neighborhood by local policemen demanding to see his papers, even though they knew him and had checked them many times before. Since 1990 there have been incidents of anti-Gypsy violence in Austria and reports of serious pogroms and persecution of Gypsies, from the Czech Republic to the Balkans, and from Romania to Italy.

Return to the entrance of Richter Höhe *and follow the road north along the left side of the* Mönchsberg.

50. Mönchsberg 18: Part of this large house belonged to Alois and Magda Grasmayr when the Nazis took power in Salzburg. Alois was a strongly anti-Nazi teacher, and their home was reportedly a frequent meeting place for Salzburgers opposed to the Nazis. The Grasmayrs provided the artist Eduard Bäumer and his family with a small apartment after the Bäumers' property had been expropriated by the Nazis. When the Nazis discovered in 1943 that Valerie Bäumer had more Jewish ancestry than they had thought, their persecution increased. Eduard was sent off to do forced labor after refusing to divorce Valarie, while eleven year old Angelica was expelled from the Hitler Youth and removed from school while being taunted and spit on by her classmates. She later recalled that it was at that moment she realized she was a Jew.

Angelica reported that when their status changed, many of their friends abandoned them, but that many others did not. Especially important were some shopkeepers and restaurant owners who took a serious risk in providing the now "Jewish" Bäumers with food (and on credit, as they had no money). Angelica also remembered that when the American bombing campaign began, her family was barred from the air raid shelter dug into the *Mönchsberg*. As Nazi Germany was being bombed and invaded by the Allies, the Nazis made a last minute effort to eliminate the remaining Jews in Germany, and the Bäumers were told that someone had seen their names on a list of people to be deported to Auschwitz. A friendly priest named Linsinger, who had promised Eduard that he would look after his family, got Valerie and her children out of Salzburg into a mountain village. There they pretended to be bombed-out—and therefore paperless—non-Jewish refugees from Vienna until the end of the War.

Continue walking north along the Mönchsberg, *and follow the footpath on the left that keeps to the edge. When you get to the overlook point north of* Neutorstrasse, *the street that comes out of the tunnel running through the* Mönchsberg, *there is an interesting information plaque about the pre-Roman settlement that was located on the slopes of the adjacent hill, called* Rainberg. *From here you can also see part of the* Riedenburg *Barracks.*

51. "Camp Judah" — Riedenburg Barracks for Displaced Persons (DP Lager Riedenburg): Right under the northwest corner of the heights of *Rainberg*, just under the wall of *Rainberg's* steep slope between *Moosstrasse* and *Leopoldskronstrasse* (where they meet *Neutorstrasse*), is the *Riedenburg* Barracks. In the summer of 1945 these barracks were turned into a Displaced Persons camp for about four hundred DPs. At first it was an assembly center organized by the US Army, but in September it was turned over to the United Nations Refugee Relief Administration, which put a Jewish veteran of the British Brigade (a unit of Jews from Palestine who fought in the British Army) in charge of the camp.

Jewish officer Jan ("Hans") Kohn of Prague and a squad of soldiers in the Riedenburg *Baracks in 1916.*

At the end of the year the Jewish residents were transferred to Munich and the camp was closed for a while. Then a mass of Jewish refugees arrived from Poland in 1946, fleeing the Antisemitic pogroms that greeted many survivors when they went home from exile, hiding, or the death camps. *Riedenburg* was reopened as "Camp Judah," and soon had over 1,800 residents. It was probably the most militant of all the DP camps.

The *Bricha* ("Flight") organization, which sent Jews illegally to Palestine, moved its headquarters here from the *Müllner* camp (see §133); and the Zionist Revisionist organization *Betar* held military training sessions here for recruits planning to fight the British and the Arabs in Palestine. *Riedenburg* was also one of the main black market centers in Salzburg, giving new fuel to Antisemitism, as the old stereotype of haggling Jewish peddlers was recycled into its new version, the "black market Jews."

In February 1947 a conflict between a rude bus driver and a Camp Judah inmate escalated into a riot. The inmate called the camp and complained that he had been thrown off the bus. It seems he had called the driver either an "SS man with SS manners" or an "SS Nazi Pig," and a crowd of angry passengers had helped the driver eject him. When the bus reached the bus stop by the camp it was met by a crowd of two hundred angry DPs. They pounded on the windows and tried to force their way onto the bus to remove the driver, provoking a free-for-all. Only the intervention of American Military Police restored order.

Camp Judah had the more usual activities too. Like most of the other camps, it had a regular school for up to a hundred and sixty children, and a religious school (*Bet Hamidrash*) that provided education for about twenty others. There was also a kindergarten for the younger children and a very well-attended night school for adults. By 1949 the Displaced Persons passing through Camp Judah were gone, and it was closed down. Sometime after the Allied Occupation, it resumed its operations as an army barracks.

Part II

♦♦♦

Across the River and Back Again

52. *State Bridge and Platzl ("Little Square")*: The State Bridge (*Staatsbrücke*) leads across the River from just outside the Town Hall Square (*Rathaus Platz*). You can see the location of the Roman and Medieval bridges a short way upstream from the State Bridge, where the gateway from the Old Market (*Altermarkt*) is visible on one side of the River and a passageway to *Steingasse* is visible on the other. A short distance to the left of the Old Market gateway is *Gehmacher's*, one of many businesses that advertised in the *Iron Broom* and kept it going.

In the late 1920s an *Iron Broom* street-seller named Lengauer regularly stood on the bridge to sell his papers. It is said that one day Walter Schwarz ran into Lengauer as he was crossing the bridge and he bought the whole bundle of Lengauer's papers and threw it into the *Salzach* River.

German soldiers march across the Staatsbrücke *during the* Anschluss *of 1938.*

A few years later, when German soldiers made their triumphant entry into Salzburg on March 12, 1938, they got a rousing reception as they marched across the bridge. Adolf Hitler got an even warmer reception from the German soldiers and the crowds when he drove across the bridge on his visit to Salzburg the following month. This was not Hitler's first visit to Salzburg. He had been here in 1912 for his army medical exam and he had attended the all-Germany meeting of the Nazi movement at the *Chiemseehof* in the 1920s (see §38 and §109).

Adolf Hitler crossing the Staatsbrücke *in April 1938.*

When German SS soldiers marched off to occupation duties in Poland in November 1939 they got a more restrained send-off at the bridge from the people of Salzburg. The Nazis had begun a project to rebuild and widen the bridge that year, using paid laborers. As the project dragged on, however, they resorted to forced laborer, including Russian POWs. The Nazis' new bridge opened for traffic in 1944, but was still unfinished when American troops rolled across on May 4, 1945, freeing the forced laborers and POWs working on the bridge. The new bridge was finally finished in 1949, and the postwar government took the credit for building it.

53. Schwartzstrasse 1: This is the *Spängler* Bank building. Like the Salzburger *Sparkasse* and *Gehmacher's*, the *Spängler* Bank advertised in the *Iron Broom*.

54. Schwarzstrasse 3 — Café Bazar: After Richard Tomaselli bought the café here in 1909 and created the *Café Bazar*, it became a popular meeting place for those associated with the nearby theaters and the Festival. Especially notable were the writers Stefan Zweig and Hugo von Hofmannsthal. In fact, Zweig held court here so regularly that table number seven became known as his table. The *Bazar* was also a favorite meeting place for many of Salzburg's Jews, and only two years after it opened, it hosted the first election meeting of the newly organized Jewish Community of Salzburg, on April 29, 1911.

A 1910 advertisement for the Café Bazar.

Sometimes the *Café Bazar* was even seen as simply a "Jewish café" by other Salzburgers. Ernst Bäck's daughter Edith Bäck Meyer wrote: "My father had a regular place in the *Café Bazar*, and he took me along often. I think the men of the 'regulars' table' were all Jewish. Perhaps a couple of others were there… He was in the *Café Bazar* daily…from one to two o'clock…that was the regulars' round." But others recall that there were two groups of regulars, one Jewish and one not, and they met at opposite ends of the *Café*. Ernst Bonyhadi recalled on his return to Salzburg with the US Army in 1945: "As soon as I got here, I went to the *Café Bazar* and the head waiter said 'Oh yes, little Ernie! I'll give you your grandfather's seat at the regulars' table.'" But after 1938 it was never again called a Jewish café.

55. *Schwarzstrasse 14:* For some years before and after 1921, at what was then *Bismarckstrasse* 14, just across from the Café Bazar, was F. Felden and Company's Vienna Fashion House (*Wiener Modehaus*).

56. *Platzl 2:* The *Blum-Haas* linoleum shop was here until it was "Aryanized" in 1938.

57. *Platzl 5/Steingasse 2:* A house on this site belonged to a Jew in the 15th century, and even in 1516, eighteen years after the 1498 expulsion, it was still referred to as a "Jews' house" (*Judenhaws*). The current structure was built in 1980.

58. *Steingasse:* This was the main residential area for Jews between their post-1404 return and their expulsion in 1498. It was the main road to the south and dates back at least to Roman times. It is often called the oldest street in Salzburg. On the right side of the Steingasse, at the corner by the Cinema (*Das Kino*), there is large scar on the wall. It seems that it was left by an American tank that got stuck here in 1945 when its crew tried to drive it all the way up the narrow street to the door of the Maison de Plaisir, a house of prostitution that can still be found just up the street, a short way past the Inner Stone Gate (*Innerer Steintor*).

59. *Steingasse 4:* This was "Fivel the Jew's House" in 1452.

60. *Steingasse 18-21:* Jewish owned properties, as early as 1429.

61. *Inner Stone Gate (Innerer Steintor) — Jews' Gate (Judentor) and Jews' Passage (Judenklause):* Jews' Gate and Jews' Passage remained the names for this gate and stretch of *Steingasse* long after their expulsion in 1498. In the 17th Century Archbishop Paris Lodron had Jews' Gate renamed St. Johannes Gate (or simply, Johannes Gate), after the St. Johannes Church on the nearby *Imbergstiege*.

62. *Steingasse 31:* From 1970 until his death in 1994 the famous Jewish Futurist Robert Jungk lived in a spacious apartment on the fourth floor of this building. David Baum, his father, whose stage name had been Max Jungk, was a well-known Berlin actor and director. Robert later took his father's stage name for his own, becoming Robert Jungk.

Robert Jungk was active in the German-Jewish and Socialist youth movements until he was forced into exile by the Nazis just before his twentieth birthday in 1933. He spent the next dozen years as an anti-Nazi journalist and activist in France, Czechoslovakia, and Switzerland. He earned a PhD while working in Zurich, but continued working as a journalist and covered the Nuremberg trials for a British paper before he moved to the US in 1948. Jungk published his first work of futurology, *The Future Has Already Begun*, in 1952, and founded an Institute for Research into the Future in Los Angeles the next year. He published his most famous book, *Brighter than a Thousand Sons*, in 1956.

Soon afterwards he returned to Europe as a peace and anti-nuclear activist. For some years he was the chairman of the Austrian Anti-Nuclear Movement, and he founded a Futurology Institute in Vienna. He was teaching in Berlin in 1970 when his high school-aged son, Peter Stefan Jungk, now a well-known author based in Paris, began to explore the counterculture. Shortly thereafter the Jungks moved to Salzburg. Peter says it was to keep him away from Berlin's hashish, which he also found available in Salzburg, however.

In any case, Robert settled in Salzburg, where he continued his leadership of the Austrian Anti-Nuclear Movement. He established a foundation and an International Futures Library in 1985, now called the Jungk Library Center (see §64). In 1991 he was the Austrian

Green Party's candidate for President, and in 1993 he was awarded the Austrian Cross of Honor for Science and Art. After his death in 1994 he was buried in the Salzburg Jewish cemetery in *Aigen*, where his wife Ruth Suschitzky Jungk joined him a few months later.

Their American-born son Peter Stefan Jungk remained in Salzburg for only a few years, until he completed his *matura* (high school diploma). Then he moved on to an international career in theater, film, and literature that took him to Switzerland, Los Angeles, Israel, Vienna, and now Paris. He is best known for his novels *Tigor* (English trans., *The Snowflake Constant*) and *Der König von Amerika* (*The King of America*), and for his 1987 biography of the author Franz Werfel.

63. Steingasse 43: Just before this house, you can see a garage dug into the *Kapuzinerberg* (Capuchins' Mountain) with the intials "F.O." and the year "1900" over the doors. It was originally dug out as a workroom for the butcher Franz Ostermaier, but it was enlarged into a large air-raid shelter in 1943 and 1944. Concentration camp prisoners (most likely political prisoners) were brought here to dig out the shelter and the two tunnels leading to it—this one and another on the far side of *Steingasse* 45—which have been used as garages since the late 1940s.

Cross the street and go down the passage leading to Imbergstrasse. Cross the street to the parking lot next to the former Imbergstrasse 2.

64. Robert Jungk Platz 1: The parking lot is now named the Robert Jungk Place, and the former *Imbergstrasse* 2 is now *Robert Jungk Platz* 1. This is the home of the Robert Jungk Foundation and Jungk Library Center.

Go back up Steingasse *to the* Imbergstiege *staircase and take it up the hill. Be sure to take advantage of the various lookout points at the top of the stairs (first right, then left) for good views of the city and the castle, before moving on to* Kapuziner Weg *(Capuchin Way).*

65. *Kapuziner Weg 5—Stefan Zweig Villa*: Across from the *Kapuziner* (*Capuchin*) Church and Cloister, this house began as a relatively modest, 17th century hunting lodge for the Archbishops of Salzburg. In the 18th century it was elongated as new rooms were added to each end and it became a far more imposing structure. It is only one room deep and has a long hall that was used for bowling during an Imperial visit in 1807. In 1918 the famous Viennese Jewish author and international peace activist Stefan Zweig was taken with the beauty of Salzburg and bought this, then dilapidated, villa on the hill overlooking the city. It looks magnificent now, but in 1919, when he and his wife moved in just after WWI, it had long been occupied only by a former gardener and her goat:

> We found our home in a nearly unlivable condition. The rain dripped freely into the rooms, and after every snowfall the hall flooded. A proper repair of the roof was impossible as the carpenters had no wood for rafters and the roofers had no lead for gutters. With difficulty the worst holes were plugged with roofing felt, but when new snow fell it did not even help when I climbed up on the roof to remove the load myself.
>
> The telephone rebelled because iron wires had been used instead of copper. We had to carry everything up the hill ourselves because nobody would deliver anything there. But the worst was the cold, as there was no coal to be had in the surrounding district, and the wood from the garden was too fresh. It hissed like a snake instead of heating, and crackled loudly instead of burning. In the emergency we turned to peat, which at least gave a semblance of heat. But for three long months I had to work in bed, writing with blue frozen fingers that I warmed under the covers after each page.
>
> But even these uncomfortable living conditions could not be complained about because the overall lack of foodstuffs and heating materials in that catastrophic year paled in the face of the housing shortage. For four years nothing had been built in Austria, many houses had collapsed, and now a numberless stream of homeless, former soldiers and prisoners of war returned. Whole families were squeezed by necessity into every available room. Commis-

sioners came to our home four times, but we had already voluntarily given up two rooms, and the inhospitable conditions and cold of our house that had seemed so hostile to us at first, protected us now; nobody else wanted to climb the hundred steps and then to freeze here.[4]

Conditions improved considerably when the roof was repaired and a modern heating system was installed. After they finished fixing up the house in the early 1920s, Zweig's wife Friderika gave him the wrought iron front gate that is still there as a birthday present.

Stefan and Friderike Zweig in their garden in the 1920s.

With the Salzburg festival drawing the world's cultural and intellectual elite to Salzburg, Zweig's villa hosted many of them. Among the writers were Thomas Mann, H.G. Wells, Hugo von Hofmannsthal, Jakob Wassermann, James Joyce, Franz Werfel, Jane Adams, Sholem Asch, and Arthur Schnitzler. The musicians included Maurice Ravel, Richard Strauss, Alban Berg, Bruno Walter, Arturo Toscanini, and Bela Bartok.

Zweig's years here from 1920 to 1933 were glorious, and he seems to have paid little mind to the Antisemitism that was rampant in Salzburg at the time, taking note of neither the Antisemitism of the Christian Social *Chronik* nor that of the *Iron Broom* in his memoirs. But after Hitler came to power in Germany, Salzburg was too close to the German border for him not to notice a change: "the agitators came across the border in cars or with mountain walking-sticks as 'simple' tourists and organized their 'cells' everywhere. They began to advertise, and also to threaten that those who did not take their side now would have to pay later."[5]

Soon old Salzburg friends turned their backs on Zweig in public for fear of being identified as a "friend of the Jews." At that point he began to think about leaving Salzburg. Then in 1934 the "Austro-fascists," led by Prime Minister Dollfuß, suspended the constitution and suppressed the Social-Democratic opposition in a short civil war. Zweig was well-known as a non-political pacifist, but early one morning he was called out of bed by two policemen so that they could "search" his house for weapons. Zweig said it was clear they did not expect to find weapons. Rather, they were sent to give him the message that he was on the new regime's enemies-list.

The next day he abandoned everything—wife, books, valuable collection of autographs, and his home—and went to England. Ownership of the villa was transferred to Friderike who chose to remain behind in Salzburg, but eventually she was forced by financial need to sell it. Because it was sold to non-Jews, the villa was never "Aryanized," but it can nonetheless be considered a property lost to Jews as a result of Antisemitism and fascism. The new owners and their successors have reportedly refused to allow any kind of memorial to Zweig on their property, but there is now a memorial across the street, in front of the *Capuchin* Cloister.

Zweig's escape to England was not enough to save him. As a stateless person and enemy alien in Britain after the beginning of WWII, and fearing that even Britain might not be able to withstand the Nazi tide, Zweig decided to move on to what he saw as a promising new world in South America. He re-settled in the multi-racial, multi-ethnic "paradise" of Rio de Janeiro in Brazil. But in the dark days of February 1942, Stefan Zweig gave up his hope for a better future even there, and committed suicide.

Visitors might want to continue up *Kapuziner Weg* past the Stefan Zweig memorial along the Cloister wall and go out along the *Stefan*

Zweig Weg for some lovely views of the Castle and the lands and mountains to the south of Salzburg. The entire way from the bottom of *Kapuziner Weg* to the top of the hill was renamed *Stefan Zweig Weg* in 1956. But the bottom section and the house numbers were left with their *Kapuziner Weg* designation after strong protests that it would be inappropriate to have this way, which is marked with the Stations of the Cross, named after a Jew. Years later the street sign at the *Linzergasse* entrance was finally revised to include the Stefan Zweig name along with the *Kapuziner Weg* designation, but the house numbers have been left unchanged.

If you are reasonably fit, proceed all the way up the hill for more impressive views and one more Kapuzinerberg *site.*

66. *Parsch and New Palestine:* Looking down from the top of the *Kapuzinerberg* behind the "Franciscans' small castle" (*Fransiskanerschlossel*) and towards the south, at the foot of the mountain called the *Gaisberg*, is the district of *Parsch*. After May 1945 the largest of Salzburg's camps for Displaced Persons was in *Parsch*, on a site directly under the steep southeast slope of the *Kapuzinerberg*, at the end facing the *Gaisberg* (where you can now see several apartment buildings). Its twenty-two barracks housed over two thousand DPs by October 1946, and even more in 1947. Most of the *Parsch* DP's in the 1940s were Jewish, though after they left, the camp was reopened for ethnic German refugees who had been expelled from Czechoslovakia, Hungary, and Romania after the German defeat. A few blocks further away from the *Kapuzinerberg* was a smaller camp with about four-hundred and fifty residents, known as New Palestine. New Palestine had a kosher kitchen and a *mikva* (ritual bath) for religious Jews. The residents also had a theater group that put on plays by Sholem Aleichem, and a lending library with some three-hundred and fifty books.

All the DP camps were largely self-governing, and members of the various Zionist organizations often led the camp councils. American

Jewish organizations like the Organization for Rehabilitation through Training (ORT) and the Hebrew Immigrant Aid Society (HIAS) set up vocational training programs to teach trades that would be useful when the residents got to Palestine. Although it was reported that ninety-nine percent of the Jewish DPs in Salzburg wanted to go to Palestine, not all of them, or even all of the most ardent Zionists among them, went. Amalie Mary Reichmann came to New Palestine after surviving stays in several concentration camps. While attending Jewish services in Salzburg she met a Jewish-American soldier named Bernard Robinson, who was active in helping the DPs.

In addition to his official duties helping the Jewish chaplain, Robinson also did things like trade American cigarettes for potatoes on the black market so he could give these potatoes (some 2,500 pounds) to the poorly organized and desperate residents of a DP camp called *Bet Trumpeldor* in the *Gnigl* district of Salzburg. Reichmann helped Robinson get false papers to bring some of his Polish relatives to Salzburg, and in the course of working together they fell in love. They married in the US in 1947.

Henrika Piencykowska was one of the women leaders of the New Palestine DP Camp and she worked closely with a Major Hamburg, a Jewish-American war crimes investigator. They too married and lived in Chicago. After the horrors of the Holocaust, family formation seemed to be a driving instinct among the DPs, and both marriage and birth rates were very high in the camps. The *Parsch* and New Palestine camps were closed in May and June of 1948 after most of the residents had left for Palestine and other destinations.

Proceed back down Kapuziner Weg *to its end at* Linzergasse, *and turn left.*

67. *Linzergasse 5:* Rudolf and Elise Fürst bought this building for their shop and home in the 19th century. After Rudolf's death in 1892 his widow ran the shop and raised her family here. Elise, who had been born in Augsburg Bavaria in 1858, was an independent and active member of the Jewish community. She was the only woman among the contributors to the new Jewish cemetery in 1893, a contribution that made it possible to move Rudolf's remains from the municipal cemetery, to become the first burial in the Jewish cemetery. In 1919 Elise led twenty other Salzburg Jews to claim Austrian citizenship in the face of a united campaign by Salzburg's Social Christians, German Nationalists, and Nazis to exclude Jews and other "non-Germans" of the former Monarchy from citizenship in the new German Austrian Republic. Two years after their campaign had failed, the same Antisemitic alliance, now with a majority on the city council, rejected a Social Democratic motion to give Nathan Kölbl "city-citizen rights" (*Bürgerrechtes*), on the grounds that Jews were not Germans and were therefore not eligible for such rights. But Kölbl was, in fact, an Austrian citizen; and Albert Pollak had been given those same rights back in 1873 (see § 69).

By 1938 *Linzergasse* 5 was owned by Elise Fürst's son, Arthur. On the street level it contained two businesses owned by members of the family: a perfume shop in Rudolf's name, but run by Arthur's sister; and Rudolf's leather goods store, which was renamed "The Tourist Shop" (*Zum Touristen*) after Arthur's wife Irene had taken it over. Arthur also had a wholesale dry goods business on the second floor, while the family lived on the third and rented out the upper floors. Martha Stein also lived here in the 1930s. She succeeded Sarah Bonyhadi as president of the Jewish Women's Society in 1932 and led the organization until it was dissolved by the Nazis.

Rudolf Fürst's leather goods shop at Linzergasse 5.
The picture was taken sometime after 1935, when Erlach's butcher shop
had opened next door. Erlach's shop is still there.

During the night and early morning hours of November 9-10, 1938, these shops were looted and destroyed, along with other Jewish properties in Salzburg—as well as Jewish properties throughout Austria and Germany. These acts of lawlessness, intimidation, and hatred soon became known as "Crystal Night" (*Reichskristallnacht*), the night of broken glass. It is often claimed that the mob in Salzburg responsible for looting and destroying Jewish properties consisted of only 30-50 members of the SA (Nazi Stormtroopers) and the Hitler Youth. That is, ordinary Salzburgers, purportedly, did not join the mob. But there is reason to doubt the claim. Irene Fürst recalled that the woman who rented their fourth floor was a Jew-hater, and her grown son had gone downstairs to break in and loot the shop on Crystal Night. Arthur said, "He broke into my house and store and destroyed everything and stole all my merchandise. This man spent his whole life in my house and as a child was always in our home and came to me with all his personal problems." Arthur also said that another man, who lived across the street, fired a gun into their apartment and later rejoiced in the destruction of that night. On the other hand, some Salzburgers actively resisted these acts of Antisemitism. Another shop owner recalled that a Catholic neighbor stood in front of his shop and discouraged the mob from destroying it by claiming that he was the new owner.

In addition to the property damage that night, forty-one Jewish men—that is, nearly all of the Jewish adult males still in the city—were beaten and arrested by SS men and the local police. They were shipped out of Salzburg, first for questioning in Vienna, and then to the concentration camp at *Dachau*. There they were "encouraged" to agree to give up their property and emigrate. Signing such a document was often a prerequisite to release from *Dachau*, just as a signed promise never to return was required for safe passage out of Salzburg in the expulsion of 1498.

Soon after the Crystal Night pogrom, *Linzergasse* 5 was "Aryanized." Irene and Arthur Fürst escaped to the US, and Irene opened a restaurant in Charleston, SC. Fifty-five years later she still waxed eloquent over the smell of a nearby cheese shop on the *Platzl*. Arthur's sister was already dying from breast cancer when the Nazis evicted her from her apartment on *Franz Josefstrasse*, and she died in Vienna before Arthur and Irene had left for America.

Ernst and Irene Löwy also lived at *Linzergasse* 5 with their teenage son Herbert, but they were not as lucky as Arthur and Irene Fürst. After leaving Salzburg they were deported to the *Theresienstadt* Ghetto concentration camp in 1942 and later murdered in *Auschwitz*. A set of small memorials called "stumbling blocks" (*Stolpersteine*) was put in the street in front of the building in 2007 in their memory.

Continue down to the end of Linzergasse. *At the* Platzl, *turn right onto* Dereifaltikeitsgasse *(Trinity Street).*

68. Dreifaltigkeitgasse 3-5: In 1938 Hermine and Max Köhler had a men's tailor shop here—it was "Aryanized" and turned over to Alois Mauracher.

69. Corner of Makartplatz and Dreifaltigkeitsgasse — Überacker-Palais: In 1856 Salzburg had been without any openly Jewish residents for over 350 years. That year a Jewish soldier named Albert Pollak from *Mattersdorf* in *Burgenland* (then part of Hungry, now Austria's easternmost province) was assigned to the Archduke Rainer Regiment that was quartered here. When his military service came to an end in 1862, Pollak got a license to trade in watches, clocks, precious metals, and antiques.

Intending to settle down in Salzburg, he rented an apartment and a shop. But then he was called into the mayor's office, and Mayor Mertens told him that Jews were not allowed to settle in Salzburg and he would have to leave. Only after Austria's new 1867 constitution guaranteed equal rights to all citizens, regardless of religion, did Albert Pollak decide to return to Salzburg and try again. This time Mayor Mertens had no choice but to allow him to stay. But he told Pollak grudgingly, "You are the first, but also the only and the last Jew in Salzburg."

But Mayor Mertens was whistling in the dark, for in 1873 his successor granted Pollak "city-citizen rights." By then Albert had already been joined by his older brother Adolf, and soon other ambitious young Jewish men joined them. They came first from the Pollaks' hometown of *Mattersdorf*, then from other towns in *Burgenland*, and then from Bohemia and Moravia (the historic Czech lands). They married Jewish women from their home areas, and by 1881 there were forty-one Jewish families in Salzburg.

By that year, the very successful Albert Pollack was living in a large combined flat and antique shop in this building with his wife and eight children. They moved out in the late 1890s after he was informed that Count Überacker no longer wanted to have Jews in his building. Later they lived on *Rainerstrasse* (see §108), overlooking the *Mirabell* Palace and the Spa Gardens. The Pollak antique business was moved there too, and among its regular customers was the Archduke Franz Ferdinand. He had Pollak honored as an official "court antiquarian," and then, in 1914, as an "imperial counselor."

Because the Pollaks were very proud of their Austrian and Salzburg identities and their military service, Albert and many other Salzburg Jews proudly wore the traditional Salzburg *Trachten* costume, something which outraged many non-Jewish Salzburgers and German nationalists. In the aftermath of their defeat in WWI, and the breakup of the Austro-Hungarian Empire, some German nationalists organized a campaign to prevent Jews from wearing this Salzburg attire. They gained considerable popular support for the campaign in the 1920s, but were unable to turn that support into law until the Nazis took power. Finally, in June of 1938, they passed the *"Trachten* Prohibition" (*Trachtenverbot*).

Albert Pollak dressed in Trachten, *the traditional native garb of Salzburgers.*

That same month Jews were also barred from public swimming pools and other facilities. In August, moreover, Jewish lawyers were stripped of the right to practice law, and Jewish doctors were prevented from treating non-Jewish patients. In 1921 Albert Pollak died an "honored citizen" (*Ehrenbürger*) of Salzburg at age 88, and the

State Governor (*Landeshauptmann*) and other officials attended his funeral. Nonetheless his widow Karoline soon moved to Vienna, saying that she found Salzburg too Antisemitic for comfort.

Albert's son Theophil Pollak in his Austrian Army uniform with his medals.

The Pollak family spread out across Austria and beyond in the next generation, and many of them escaped the Holocaust. Albert and Karoline's oldest daughter Irma married a Regimental doctor named Herz who later served on the Austrian General Staff. This proved no protection during the Holocaust and Irma was killed in *Theresienstadt* in 1942. After having survived *Theresienstadt* and *Bergen-Belsen*, Irma's daughter Mini Herz found herself the last living member of her family in Europe in 1945.

Karoline Pollak in her later years.

70. *The Makartplatz (Makart Square):* This square was named after Hans Makart, a famous Salzburg painter who died in 1886. In the mid-1930s it was renamed *Dollfuß* Square in honor of Austrian Chancellor Engelbert Dollfuß. Dollfuß closed the parliament in 1933 and crushed the Socialists in a short civil war in 1934. He turned Austria into a dictatorhip, often called "Austro-fascist," because of its resemblance and close ties to Mussolini's fascist Italy. Soon after this, Dollfuß was murdered by Nazis during an attempted coup d'etat, and his followers transformed him into a martyr for Austrian independence.

Since Dollfuß had addressed a rally on this square shortly before his assasination, it was renanmed in his honor. But when the Hilter took over Austria in 1938, the local Nazis renamed the square the *Adolf-Hitler-Platz*. Hitler rejected the honor and had the square restored to its original name, *Makartplatz*. Dollfuß is still considered a national martyr by the Austrian Peoples' Party today, a designation that is hotly contested by the Social Democrats and the Greens.

Changing street signs in 1938: "Dollfuß Platz" *becomes* "Adolf-Hilter-Platz."

Proceed down the left side of the square.

71. Makartplatz 7: This had been the Salzburg headquarters of the Austrian Touring-Club, before it was taken over by the Austro-Fascists and used as the Salzburg headquarters for their "Fatherland Front" in the mid-1930s. The Nazis occupied it on the night of March 11, 1938, and used it as the headquarters for their seizure of power in Salzburg. Later it became the official Nazi Party headquarters for Salzburg.

Occupation of the "House of the Fatherland Front," March 12, 1938

72. Makartplatz 8: The offices of two prominent Jewish attorneys, Dr. Julius Pollak and Dr. Franz Grün were here in the 1930s. The two attorneys lived in houses that Julius Pollak owned on *Wiesbauerstrasse* (see §137) until Dr. Pollak fled to Montevedeo with his family after the 1938 Annexation. A few months later, Dr. Grün was forced out of Salzburg, and both the homes and the offices were "Aryanized."

73. Makartplatz 1: Until 1938 this housed the dental workshop of Erich Zeilinger. Then the workshop was "Aryanized."

74. Schwarzstrasse 5-7: Built in 1866 as the Hotel Austria (*Hotel d'Autriche*), this was and remains one of Salzburg's great hotels. It is currently called the Hotel *Sacher*. When the Salzburg Festival began in the 1920s, it was a social center for its organizers, and Max Reinhardt, Hugo von Hofmansthal, and Richard Strauss stayed here. In later years it was regularly host to Bruno Kreisky, Austria's only Jewish Chancellor.

Indeed, no less an author than Jean Amery chose this site to end his life. Born in Austria as Hans Meyer ("Amery" is an anagram for Meyer), he was captured and tortured by the *Gestapo* as a member of the Belgian Resistance. He was sent to *Auschwitz* and then *Bergen-Belsen*. After the war he returned to Austria and became famous in literary circles, only to commit suicide here in 1978.

In 1988 the hotel was taken over by the owners of Vienna's Hotel *Sacher* and renamed. A *Café Sacher* was installed on the street level with a lovely terrace overlooking the river. It is well worth visiting for a taste of its much imitated, but never equaled, world famous *Sacher Torte*.

75. *Schwarzstrasse 13:* In the early years of the 20th century this building contained the home of Ignaz Glaser and his family. As the name suggests, Glaser came from a family that had been involved in glass making for a long time, as had the family of his wife Emmy Kupfer Glaser. In 1881 Ignaz moved from Bohemia to the village of *Bürmoos*, just north of Salzburg, to take over a bankrupt glass factory. He rapidly rebuilt this factory into a large and successful operation, making him the only major industrialist among Salzburg's Jews, and one of the few major industrialists in the entire Salzburg region.

An aerial sketch of Glaser's factory.

A few years after their son Hermann was born in 1890, Emmy and Hermann Glaser moved to Salzburg to escape the social isolation of the working class and Catholic *Bürmoos*. As a major industrialist, Ignaz and his family were in a class above the rest of Salzburg's Jewish community, but Ignaz was nonetheless active in establishing both the Jewish cemetery in *Aigen* and the *Lasserstrasse* Synagogue. Like most industrialists, he was a German National Liberal in politics until the rising Antisemitism of the late 19th century caused him to shift his allegiances. Until 1897 he was a member of the liberal Salzburger Gymnastic Union (*Männerturnverein*), which had long refused to exclude Jews from membership. But he and the other Jewish members were expelled that year when it, too, adopted an "Aryans only" membership clause.

As the Christian Socials were even more openly Antisemitic than the Liberals, Glaser shifted his support to the only party that clearly opposed Antisemitism, the Social Democratic Party. In this way he became something of a paradox: a wealthy capitalist supporting a party committed to ending capitalism. Indeed, even as he was giving his support to the Social Democrats politically, Glaser bought a title of nobility in 1909, making him a Knight of the Franz-Josef Order

(*Ritter des Franz-Josef-Ordens*). This led his 19-year old son Hermann to write in his diary, "the title of nobility always helps in some circles, and the Salzburg Antisemites will turn green with envy."

Ignaz Glaser.

This son, Hermann, left Salzburg for a few years to study in Vienna. After earning a doctorate in 1912, he returned to Salzburg and the family business. Just before the outbreak of the WWI, his father opened a new factory in the soft coal region of Moravia. He died there on August 11, 1916, and was buried in the Jewish cemetery in *Aigen*. When Austria-Hungary was dismantled by the victorious allies after the war, Hermann and his family moved to Czechoslovakia where their more modern production facilities were located, leaving a cousin in charge of the *Bürmoos* operation. But the division of Austria-Hungary was an economic disaster that led to the bankruptcy of many businesses, including that of the Glasers in 1926.

Ignaz Glaser's memorial in the Jewish Cemetery.

In 1938 Hermann returned to Salzburg where he became an insurance agent, living in much reduced circumstances at *Faberstrasse* 30. In November of that year he was rounded up along with the other Jewish men of Salzburg, winning his release from *Dachau* only after promising to leave the *Reich* and to give up a house in *Grödig* that he had inherited from his mother. On his release Hermann made his way to Shanghai, but he returned to Vienna in 1947, where he set up a successful glass business. After his death in 1956, his body was returned to Salzburg and buried near those of his parents in the Jewish cemetery in *Aigen*.

Although the Glasers have long been gone from Bürmoos, *Ignaz Glaser was not forgotten. The main street running through the small town is named* Ignaz Glaser Strasse.

76. Schwarzstrasse 24-28 — The Mozarteum: In 1880 the *Mozarteum* (Mozart Foundation) was established to promote fine music. The foundation acquired the *Villa Lasser* on this site for a music center, research library, and school. Over the years the *Villa Lasser* became too small and was replaced by a magnificent concert hall in the early 20th century.

A 1941 letterhead for the Mozarteum, *renamed "The Empire's College for Music," with a Nazi eagle and swastika.*

The new hall hosted many wonderful concerts, but also public meetings like the German People's Day (*Deutsche Volkstag*) celebration on May 26, 1918. This was organized by the German Freedom and Christian Social parties and was "for Germans (Aryans) only." The speakers denounced the alleged Jewish domination of Austria and called for the elimination of Jews from the universities, saying that the monarchy had "privileged a band of thieves." Cannon Daniel Etter, representing the Christian Social State Governor (*Landeshauptmann*), brought down the house when he said, "The Jews themselves are already "cut" [i.e., circumcised], but it is very important to "cut" their moneybags as well, before Israel can rob everything from our State and people."

Hitler's birthday celebration in the Mozarteum, *April 22, 1941.*

Despite this use by Antisemites, the *Mozateum* continued for many years as a music academy for many of the children of Salzburg's Jewish community—like the opera singer Erwin Bonyhadi. In 1938, however, the Nazis took it over, and in the early 1940s they promoted the *Mozarteum* as the *Reich's* premier music school. The Mozarteum also hosted a major wartime assembly of Nazi regional governors (*Gauleiters*).

Nazi regional governors' meeting in the Mozarteum.

After the war, with the arrival of refugees and Holocaust survivors, Salzburg had thousands of Jews for the first time in its history. They needed a large hall for their religious observances, and so the *Mozarteum* was pressed into service. Amalie Mary Reichmann from the New Palestine DP Camp met her future husband, the Jewish-American soldier Bernard Robinson, while attending Jewish services here. Since the late 1940s, the *Mozarteum* has again served as a concert hall and music school, maintaining the highest of standards and achieving world renown in both endeavors.

77. *Schwarzstrasse 22 — The City Theater/State Theater:* This magnificent theater opened as the City Theater (*Stadttheater*) in October 1893. The then obscure actor Max Reinhardt played here during its opening season. It was the presence of facilities like the City Theater and the *Mozarteum* that inspired Reinhardt to dream of creating a major event for German theater, music, and the arts in Salzburg — the Salzburg Festival.

In August 1939 Adolf Hitler and Martin Bormann attended the theater here and enjoyed a performance, but Hitler criticized the theater's color scheme. It was soon changed to suit his taste. The

Nazis elevated the theater's status from a mere "City" Theater (*Stadttheater*) to a "State" Theater (*Landestheater*), and Goebbels' Ministry of Propaganda subsidized it heavily until it was closed in the last year of WWII.

Adolf Hitler (left center) and Martin Bormann (far right, looking into the camera) in the City Theater.

In 1945 the City Theater's former director, Egon Hilbert, returned from seven years of imprisonment in a concentration camp to briefly resume his directorship. He began with the production of long-banned plays. There were also some new plays produced, as with the May 1946 opening of Arthur Becker's play about life in the *Mauthausen* Concentration Camp.

On August 21, 1960, the Salzburg Jewish Community and Jewish groups from Vienna organized a celebration of the 100th anniversary of Theodor Herzl's birth. It was presided over by the Chief Rabbi from Vienna, Dr. Akiba Eisenberg, and celebrated in the Salzburg State Theater. Numerous local and provincial notables were invited to attend, including the Provincial Governor (*Landeshauptmann*), members of the Salzburg provincial legislature, the Mayor of Salzburg, the members of the city council, the president of the Salzburg Festival Society, and the Director of the Festival. The inventive ways that these men found to excuse themselves from attending the celebration make for amusing reading: the Provincial Governor was "on vacation," the Mayor was scheduled to be in *Carinthia*, a councilman had to be in Frankfort for the day, and so on, and so forth.

78. *Makartplatz 4 — The Hotel Bristol:* Another of Salzburg's grand hotels from the turn of the last century was the 1894 Hotel Electric-Works — the first hotel in the city with electric lights. It boasted a mural by the painter Hans Makart on the left side of the main reception hall that is still there. Soon renamed the Hotel Bristol, it was Sigmund Freud's favorite place to stay when he came to Salzburg, and he arranged for it to host one of the major conventions of the Society for Psychoanalysis.

In October 1923 a birthday party for the prominent Jewish matron Sarah Bonyhardi, scheduled for the Spa, had to be cancelled when the *Iron Broom* threatened disorders. The management of the Hotel Bristol allowed it to be rescheduled there for November 3, after the Republican Guard (the Socialist Party militia) offered to provide security.

The party was sponsored by the Salzburg Jewish Women's Society, and about a hundred people, including children, were enjoying the party when two groups of about forty Nazis each marched on the hotel shouting, "Salzburgers Awake!", and various other Nazi slogans. One of the groups tried to break into the hotel to disrupt the party, but the men of the Republican Guard kept them out and the party proceeded undisturbed. The Republican Guard was later crushed by the "Austro-fascists" in the civil war of 1934. In 1938 the German Army took over the Hotel Bristol and made it their General Headquarters (*Generalkommando*) for the region. Later they moved the Headquarters to the larger and even more elaborate Hôtel de l'Europe (see §121) near the railroad station.

Hotel Bristol as General Headquarters for the German Army.

One of the shops to the right of the entrance to the Hotel Bristol was the site of Friedrich Pasch's first shoe store in the late 19th century. Then known as the *Niederlage der K.k. Münchengrätzer Schuhfabrik*, it was later called, simply, the *Pasch* Shoe Store (*Schuhhaus Pasch*), and grew into a chain of six stores across Austria.

From 1921 to 1938 Solomon Eisenberg had a clothing store in the Bristol building, but it did not survive the Nazis' anti-Jewish boycott. During the occupation after WWII, the hotel served as headquarters for the American Occupation Forces.

From the Bristol go back to Dreifaltigkeitsgasse *and cross the street. Go left to* Bergstrasse *and follow it back towards* Linzergasse.

79. *Bergstrasse 8:* Daniel Bonyhadi started off in business with a shoemaker's supply shop here in the late 1890s (see §111).

Continue to Linzergasse, *and turn left.*

80. *Linzergasse 20:* Adolf Kohn opened a clothing shop here in 1883. Soon he had a relative named Max Kohn working for him, and they became partners here by the end of the century. A few years later Max had his own shop and Adolf listed his wife Ida as his business partner. He was still advertising his business here at least through 1907, and possibly until 1910, when the entire street-level of the building was converted into the *Guggentaler Stübl* (beer hall). In 1914 Adolf died at the age of 56; but Ida lived to see her 75th birthday, dying in Salzburg in 1931.

81. *Linzergase 26*: Franziska Kohn had her tailoring shop here during the 1880s and 1890s.

82. *Linzergasse 28*: The "Tourist Shop" clothing store (*Zum Touristen*), owned by master tailor Theodor Kurtz, was here from the mid-1890s until 1938. It was placed on the *Iron Broom*'s list of Jewish businesses to be boycotted in 1923, and it was reportedly looted in 1938, although it does not appear on the lists of properties that were "Aryanized" by the Nazis. Theodor's widow, Maria, recalled in 1953 that after the Annexation the anti-Jewish boycott, with "SS Men" stationed in front of the store to discourage customers, was so effective that business had virtually ceased. (Photos from the time, however, show that it was SA Stormtroopers rather than SS Men who enforced the boycott.)

Theodor Kurz stands in front of his shop at Linzergasse *28.*

Maria took the elderly Theodor to Vienna to protect him from the uproar. As a result it was their son who was rounded up in Salzburg on Crystal Night rather than Theodor. But Theodor was soon taken into custody in Vienna anyway. Maria was able to win the release of their son, but not the elderly and frail Theodor. Becoming very ill from the shock of his arrest and the abuse he suffered in the Vienna prison, Theodor died in prison.

Horse-drawn trolly car with "Tourist Shop" advertisement. The sign reads:"Best and cheapest source for Men's and Children's clothing."

83. *Linzergasse 48:* Owned by Gisela "Pierag" (probably "Pirak"—see §85), this building was "Aryanized" in 1938. It is now the *Goldene Krone* (Golden Crown) Hotel.

84. *Linzergasse 52:* Josef Sagel's shop here, "Low-Price Sagel" (*Kleinpreis Sagel*), was "Aryanized" in 1938 and taken over by Max Dillinger. Whether or not this Dillinger was related to his contemporary, the famous American bank robber John Dillinger, is unknown.

85. *Linzergasse 53 and Wolf Dietrichstrasse 2:* In the 1920s Leopold Pirak had a second-hand shop here and lived upstairs with his family. By 1938 Leopold had died, but his seventy-year old widow, Gisela Pirak, and her daughter Erna continued to live upstairs, above the *Wolf Dietrichstrasse* entrance. The apartment was "Aryanized" that year, along with the Pirak's clothing store around the corner (on the *Linzergasse* side), and they were forced to flee Salzburg.

86. *Schallmooserhauptstrasse 6:* Amalie and Florentine Rosenfeld lived in the first floor apartment of this building until it was "Aryanized" in November 1939. The apartment was taken over by the SS-Man Hans Schwarzenbacher and his wife. After the war, Schwarzenbacher was imprisoned for a while in Camp Orr/*Lager Glasenbach*, the special SS and Nazi Prison camp.

87. *Schalmooserhauptstrasse 6a:* This street-level shop belonged to the "half-Jewish" Otto Scheck and his brother. It was "Aryanized" in 1938 along with the home of Otto and his wife Helene at *Rennbahnstrasse* 11, located on the other side of the *Kapuzinerberg* (Capuchins' Mountain) and south of the *Volksgarten*, near the racetrack (*Rennbahn*). As Otto bitterly recalled, SA Stormtroopers "immediately confiscated my BMW motorcycle."

Continue walking on the left side of Schalmooserhauptstrasse *to* Bayerhammerstrasse; *turn left and go one block to the start of* Lasserstrasse.

88. *Lasserstrasse 6:* This was the site of a rented prayer room for the Jewish community in the late 19th century.

89. *Lasserstrasse 8:* With the re-creation of a growing Jewish community in the late 19th century, a place to hold services was needed. A Salzburg branch of the larger Jewish Community of Linz, about an hour and a half away in Upper Austria, was established and rented quarters for services in Salzburg. Originally they were in the *Sternbräu* building between *Getreidegasse* and *Griesgasse*. Later these services were moved to a room in *Lasserstrasse* 6, and then to one in the *Schiesslerhaus* on *Getreidegasse*.

In 1897 the congregation got its first rabbi, Dr. Moses Bach, and no longer had to depend on occasional visits from the Linz rabbis. By the end of the century there were over thirty Jewish families associated with the Salzburg branch of the Linz community, and they set up a Temple Construction Committee. For a long time it was impossible to find anyone who would sell land to the Committee, so in June 1901 the head of the Committee, Professor Gottlieb Winkler from the trade school, bought the parcel at *Lasserstrasse* 8 in his own name.

But the Committee's challenges were not at an end. In the late 19th century the Antisemitism that had weakened in the middle of the century once again grew stronger in Austria with the formation of newly active Antisemitic organizations. In 1894 the Antisemitic "United Christians," led by Adolf Stainer, won control of the Salzburg district council. Strainer's was nickname was "the Salzburg Lueger," after the famous Antisemitic Mayor of Vienna, Karl Lueger. Thus it was no surprise that the Salzburg authorities resisted granting a construction permit for a synagogue. They finally approved a plan for building it at the rear of the property after they forced the Committee to give up its plan to put the synagogue directly on the street. In September 1901, on *Rosh Hashanah* (the Jewish New Year), the building was ready for services.

By 1911 the Salzburg Jewish Community had grown to about eighty families and 285 individuals, and the brilliant and forceful Dr. Adolf Altmann had come to Salzburg to be their rabbi. That year, as well, it finally achieved its long-standing goal of becoming legally independent of the Linz Jewish Community. Needing government approval for this, the leaders had been previously blocked by the Salzburg authorities' insistence that they were too few in number to support an independent society. Surprisingly, however, their request for an independent society was now backed by Julius Sylvester, who had been a major figure in bringing the new German nationalist Antisemitic campaign to Salzburg in the 1880s.

After Austria's defeat in WWI and the creation of the first Austrian Republic, Antisemitism grew still stronger and more virulent. The Jews of Salzburg became socially even more isolated in the 1920s and 1930s. The Jewish Community continued as an independent society until the Annexation and Nazi take-over of 1938, but it had already shrunk to 239 members.

Like most other synagogues in the Third *Reich*, this one was attacked and looted during the Crystal Night pogrom, though it was too close to the neighboring buildings to be burned down. Salzburg's Rabbi David Margulies fled to England with his wife after he was released from *Dachau*, and the ruins of the synagogue were taken over by the Nazi's *Organization Todt* (named for Fritz Todt) for a storage depot, while ownership was transferred to the German police.

Rabbi and Mrs. Margulies in England after his release from Dachau.

As German government property, the building was taken over by the American occupation forces in August of 1945. In July 1946 the Provincial Salzburg government offered to "give" the ruined synagogue back to the Salzburg Jewish community. In 1959 a *mikva* (ritual bath) was rebuilt in the cellar, and between 1967 and 1968 the synagogue itself was restored and reopened. Many local officials attended the reopening ceremony on December 11, 1968, including Salzburg's Archbishop Andreas Rohracher.

US Sergeant Ernest Bonyhadi in front of the ruined Synagogue in 1945.

In November 1985 a memorial to Jews who had been persecuted and expelled from Salzburg between 1938 and 1945 was dedicated in the synagogue garden. There was some criticism of the decision to place it behind a hedge rather than in a more conspicuous location. Salzburg's major newspaper, the *Salzburger Nachrichten* commented: "Will nobody except the members of the Jewish Community see it? Then it will remind nobody of the cruelties... inflicted by the citizens of Salzburg on their fellows."[6] But the painting of a large Jewish star on the house of the stonecutter who had made the memorial suggests that these security concerns were not misplaced.

Unveiling of the memorial for the 1938 destruction of the synagogue and the victims of the Holocaust.

Rabbi David Nussbaum, a Lubavitcher rabbi from the United States, came to Salzburg and served the congregation from 1990 to 2001. He was its only full-time rabbi since the flight of Rabbi Margulies in 1938. But in 2001 he was dismissed in the course of a dispute with Community President Marko Feingold. At present (at the writing of this *Guide*), the synagogue continues to operate without a rabbi, except on major holidays, when one comes in from Vienna. Services continue to be held every Saturday morning.

Continue on Lasserstrasse *to* Stelzhammerstrasse; *go left, and then left again onto* Franz Josefstrasse. *From there, continue to* Vierthalerstrasse *and turn right.*

90. *Vierthalerstrasse 8:* This was Rabbi Altmann's home in 1914 when he was called into military service during WWI.

Continue on Vierthalerstrasse *to* Wolf-Dietrichstrasse, *and turn right.*

91. *The Witches' Tower—Southwest Corner of Wolf Dietrichstrasse and Paris Lodronstrasse:* By the early 20th century this was the last surviving tower of the late 15th century city wall. Used as one of the city's prisons, it was called the Witches' Tower (*Hexenturm*) because accused witches were confined here before being burned. Witches as well as Jews had been burned in Salzburg long before this tower was built, but the burning of Jews had ended by the time Salzburg authorities began to hold witches here.

The burning of witches peaked in the 17th century when nearly one hundred persons, mostly young begger boys, were killed in the witch hunt of 1678-79. (Some ten years later, the famous witch hunt in the much smaller Salem, Massachusetts, took nearly as many lives.) Archbishop Colloredo finally prohibited the hunting and burning of alleged witches in 1778. The tower continued to be used as a prison on and off until 1804, and it was finally destroyed by an American bombing raid in November 1944. A new building was erected here in 1969, and a memorial to the Witches' Tower was placed on the wall of the building.

Continue down Wolf Dietrichstrasse *into the* St. Andrä Quarter.

92. St. Andrä Quarter: This quarter of Salzburg (indicated on the map by the dotted line) surrounds the new *St. Andrä* Church (located at the number 92), which was built across the street from the *Mirabell* Palace in the 1890s to replace an older *St. Andrä* Church on the *Platzl*. Most of the buildings in this quarter date from the expansion of Salzburg in this direction in the late 19th century. By the early 20th century it had become the main Jewish quarter in Salzburg—not that most of its residents were Jewish, but most of the city's Jews lived in this quarter.

93. Wolf Dietrichstrasse 14—Northeast corner of Wolf Dietrichstrasse and Paris Lodronstrasse: This was the home of Cantor and religion teacher Hermann Kohn and his wife Berta when it was "Aryanized" in 1938 and they were forced to leave Salzburg. Their kosher restaurant was at *Haydnstrasse* 10 (see §101).

Continue down Wolf Dietrichstrasse *to* Schrannengasse; *go left on* Schrannengasse *to the intersection with* Haydnstrasse *and look to the right.*

94. Haydnstrasse 2: This included Ernst Bäck's flour and groceries importing agency and his apartment, which were originally located at Faberstrasse 11. In 1938 they were "Aryanized," although by that time Ernst himself no longer lived there. He had been captured as a soldier in the Austrian Army and died in a Siberian POW camp in 1920.

After WWII, Marko Feingold and other Jewish survivors took over the first floor of this building, which had been the headquarters of a Nazi women's organization during the War. They lived here and set up a center for assisting Displaced Persons, or "DPs."

95. *Haydnstrasse 5:* This 1938 address is now included in Haydnstrasse 1, the original buildings having been replaced after the WWII bombings. A Jewish widow named Margarethe Wraubek rented an apartment here until it was "Aryanized" in 1938.

Turn back and face the other side of Schrannengasse.

96. *Schrannengasse 10—Franz Josef Kaserne and Camp Herzl:* This was a former Austrian army barracks named after Emperor Franz Josef. In June 1946 it was re-opened to serve as the main reception center for DPs after the occupation authorities decided to close the earlier center in the bomb-damaged Hotel Europa (§121). The center was called Camp *Herzl*, and for over a year it stood as a shining example of how *not* to run a DP camp. It was overcrowded, having entirely inadequate facilities for its up to 2,000 residents.

Red Cross food distribution in the Franz Josef Barracks, DP Camp Herzl.

When the US authorities decided to shut down the camp in the summer of 1947, they failed to communicate their plans to the residents. That is, at least they failed to adequately reassure the camp residents that they were not planning something terrible. The residents, who had survived the death camps and returned home to pogroms in their homelands before fleeing to Salzburg, panicked, barricaded themselves in the camp and went on a hunger strike. Two hundred American soldiers sent to remove them used tear gas and maintained a week-long siege before the situation was resolved.

Walk further down Schrannengasse *to* Mirabellplatz *and turn left.*

97. Mirabellplatz 6: Ludwig "Leon" Abrahamer had a tailor shop here by 1894. Before the end of the decade he developed it into a branch of a Vienna clothing store called "The Sailor's Place" (*Zum Matrosen*), which also had branches in *Linz* and *Innsbruck*. After he died, the store was taken over by his widow and their son Julius, who continued the business until it was "Aryanized" in 1938.

*Newspaper ad for "The Sailor's Place" (*Zum Matrosen*).*

In the 1920s Oswald Löwy had opened a souvenir shop next door, but at the same address. The souvenir shop was still owned by his son Paul when the Nazis took over. Isidor Fuchs and Manfried Bonyhadi also had their Fuchs and Co. shop here in the 1920s, before they moved it across the river to *Getreidegasse* 21 (§19).

Paul Löwy in the doorway of his shop during the 1938 boycott. A Nazi Stormtrooper stands by.

Continue to Paris-Lodronstrasse.

98. *Paris-Lodronstrasse 2:* When this site was excavated for construction in 1872, the workers found a buried hoard of over 2,300 Roman coins. These dated back to the 241 CE invasion by the Germanic Alemanns. (Alemannic still survives today in German dialects spoken in Switzerland and Austrian *Vorarlberg*.) In the 1930s this was the site of the enlarged *Pasch* Shoe Store (*Schuhhaus Pasch*), which had begun in the Hotel Bristol building (see §78). After Friedrich's death in 1934, his widow Adele Pasch and their children Grete and Hans became the owners of the largest shoe store in Salzburg, with a chain of six stores across Austria. It was Grete who actually ran the business.

Adele, Hans and Grete Pasch.

In 1938 Hans Pasch was sent to *Dachau* and the *Pasch* Shoe Store was "Aryanized" and turned over to Nazi party members Sepp Fischer and Georg Mathies. The Paschs made their way to England, and Hans eventually settled in Denver, Colorado, where he said the mountains reminded him of Austria.

Stromtroopers at their posts during the 1938 boycott of the Pasch *Shoe Store*

Max Köhler also lived at this address in the 1930s. He was the head of the Salzburg branch of the Union of Austrian Jews (*Union Österreichisher Juden*) for about five years after its founding in 1930.

Go along Paris-Lodronstrasse *a short way, and turn left onto* Faberstrasse.

99. *Faberstrasse 8 (on the right, before Hubert Sattlergasse):* The *Andrä* School complex included the leading High School in Salzburg. Many of the Jewish children of the early 20th century attended these schools, as did the famous, non-Jewish Austrian playwright Thomas Bernhard. Bernhard wrote in his memoirs that the teachers were mostly Nazis even before 1938; and that the Catholic teachers after the war were cut from the same cloth. On the building wall is a plaque commemorating Albert Einstein's physics lecture here on September 21, 1909. After WWII, Marko Feingold arranged for the gymnasium to be used as an overnight shelter for DPs until better quarters could be found.

Turn right onto Hubert Sattlergasse.

100. *Hubert Sattlergasse 13:* Adolf Jacoby was born in the Württemberg region of south-western Germany, but came to Salzburg as a young man to work for a cousin named Albert Levi. He began as a peddler with a horse and wagon, traveling through the villages of the *Tirol* and *Vorarlberg* in western Austria, but eventually became Levi's office manager. He lived here on the first floor with his wife Emilie and his son Hans.

In 1926 Emilie died and Hans moved out. Adolf continued here alone, with a housekeeper, until he was nearly 80 years old and with just one leg. By then he was the retired manager of a nearby textile and furniture wholesale business. In 1938 his apartment was "Aryanized" and he emigrated to Holland to join his son. Adolf died in an old age home in 1943. His son, Hans Jacoby, survived the German occupation in hiding and later wrote an autobiography in Dutch.

During the Nazi years the "Aryanized" Jacoby apartment had been turned over to SS Assault Troop leader (*Sturmbann-führer*) Hermann Höfle and his family. Born in Salzburg in 1911, Höfle joined the Nazi Party in 1933 and began his SS career even before the Annexation. He became one of Adolf Eichmann's leading associates after attracting Eichmann's attention by his "efficient management" of the 1938 Crystal Night pogrom in Salzburg. The apartment was thus one of his rewards for a "pogrom well done."

After attending the Nazi Leadership School (*Führer-schule*) in *Dachau*, Höfle rose rapidly, and in 1943 he was promoted to Chief-of-Staff for fellow Austrian Odilo Globocnik, the SS and Police Commander in *Lublin*, Poland, during the Holocaust. Höfle was put in charge of Operation Reinhard and directed the deportations from the *Lublin*, *Lemberg*, and *Warsaw* Ghettos to the death camps of *Belzec*, *Sobibór*, and *Treblinka*.

Eichmann testified that Höfle was the one who set up the gas chambers at several of the death camps; and in a message to Eichmann, Höfle boasted of the elimination of one-and-a-half million Jews by Operation Reinhard. In May 1945 Höfle was imprisoned in the British POW camp at *Wolfsberg* in *Carinthia*, where he was photographed next to the body of his fomer chief Odilo Globocnik, after Globocnik escaped justice by committing suicide. In August 1947 Höfle was turned over to the Austrian authorities, who released him two months later. When the Polish government requested his extradition in 1948 for mass murder, he went into hiding in Italy. By 1951, however, he was back in Salzburg, having learned that Cold War era US authorities would not extradite accused war criminals to Communist countries.

A few years later Höfle was hired by American military intelligence in Bavaria and provided with a false identity. The job only lasted a year, but his false papers remained useful. Finally, after being named as a leading perpetrator by Eichmann in 1961, Höfle was arrested in Salzburg where he was working in his old trade as an auto mechanic for the city water department. Just before Höfle was due to go on trial for war crimes, Eichmann was executed and Höfle committed suicide in a jail in Vienna.

Shortly after the war, the resistance fighter and former *Dachau* and *Buchewald* political prisoner, Guido Kopp, moved into the Jacobys' old apartment. After his death, his wife remained there until her death in 2002. Hans Jacoby said she was very gracious to him and his son when they visited Salzburg in 1993. A Jewish presence was maintained in the building for yet another three years when the author of this *Guide* moved into a third floor apartment shortly before the widow's death.

101. *Haydnstrasse 10:* From 1912 to 1938 this was a kosher restaurant belonging to Cantor Hermann Kohn of the Lasserstrasse synagogue and his wife Berta. It was said that Hermann had a wonderful singing voice, but he needed more than that to support his family. Thus, with the support of Rabbi Altmann and the Jewish community, the couple sought a permit to open Salzburg's first kosher restaurant in March 1911. The Restaurant Owners' Association opposed the permit, however, and the city authorities followed their recommendation, based on the claim that Salzburg already had more than enough restaurants. Moreover, the Salzburg authorities were unimpressed with the argument that the only kosher restaurant in the entire province of Salzburg was in far away *Bad Gastein*, while the nearest kosher restaurants were an hour or more away across the German border.

After exhausting the local and provincial appeals processes, the Kohns finally appealed to the Ministry of Commerce in Vienna, who, as in the past, overturned Salzburg's attempt to restrict Jewish affairs. On December 6, 1911, the Ministry ordered the city of Salzburg to issue a permit for Cantor Kohn to open a kosher restaurant, which he did on January 13, 1912. The Nazis ordered the restaurant closed on October 28, 1938.

Go back across Hubert Sattlergasse *to* Franz-Josef-Strasse, *and turn left.*

102. Franz-Josef-Strasse 12: In 1938 the widow Amalie Löwy lived on the second floor with her son Robert, his wife Lydia, and their young son. A first floor apartment belonged to Emilie and Ludwig Fischer (partners in Fischer and Aninger, see §13), and their son Walter. That year both apartments were "Aryanized" and these families were evicted. The Fischer's apartment was taken over by the German *Reich* Labor Service.

103. Franz-Josef-Strasse 8: Several Jewish families lived here before the "Aryanization." Alice and Otto Löwy lived in the first floor apartment before they fled to Latin America and their apartment was turned over to a Nazi "Banner-leader" (*Standartenfüher*) named Lothar, and his family. Manfred and Else Bonyhadi, with "little Ernie" and their other children, shared a large second floor apartment with Manfred's sister Martha and his brother-in-law and business partner Isidor Fuchs (of Fuchs and Company, see §19). Their apartment was taken over by a family named Vogl. The apartment of Wilhelm Popper was also "Aryanized."

Return to Faberstrasse *and turn right.*

104. Faberstrasse 11: In 1911 this was the home of Rabbi Adolf Altmann, and it was listed in the Salzburg directory as the headquarters for the Society for Jewish History and Literature. The society had been founded in 1902, and by 1911 it had 22 members. It peaked at 32 members in 1914 when Rabbi Altmann and several others were called into wartime service, at which point the society suspended operations, never to resume them.

In 1938 Rebekka and Julius Klüger lived on the first floor with their son Severin. Their apartment was "Aryanized" and given over to the Red Cross, while they escaped to the US. Antique dealers Bela and Therese Spiegel lived in a third floor apartment with Bela's brother Ladislaus, who ran another small shop. The Spiegels' shop, at *Getreidegasse* 34, was looted during the Crystal Night pogrom (see

§23). Before the Spiegels had moved in, the apartment was the home, and flour and grocery import agency of Ernst Bäck, who had founded the business early in the 20th century at *Faberstrasse* 9. After several years at this location he moved his family and the business to *Haydnstrasse* 2 (see §94).

After the Spiegels' apartment was "Aryanized," it was turned over to a Nazi Block-Leader named Holzleitner, along with Frau Karla Seebald and her grandmother. Seebald was the secretary of Combat-commander Chief (*Kampfkommandanten Oberst*) Hans Lepperdinger, the official who surrendered Salzburg to the American forces without a fight in May 1945.

105. *Faberstrasse* 7: In the 1920s and 1930s Josef and Erna Schönhorn lived here with their son Martin on the ground floor. In 1926 Josef became the founding leader of the Zionist Local of Salzburg (*Zionistiche Ortsgruppe Salzburg*) and retained that position until Walter Schwarz took over around 1930. The apartment was "Aryanized" and turned over to the Red Cross in 1938, while the Schönhorns escaped to South America.

Turn right onto Hubert Sattlergasse.

106. *Hubert Sattlergasse* 7: Anna Maria Wahl lived here before she was institutionalized. She was one of the more than 70,000 handicapped Germans whose lives were declared "worthless" by Adolf Hitler (who had a visceral hatred of people "who habitually dirtied themselves" and "put their own excrement in their mouths as if it were food").[7] They were among the first victims of the Nazis' newly invented gas chambers between 1939 and 1941. Wahl was murdered at Hartheim Castle outside Linz, only an hour and a half from home. In 2007 a "stumbling block" (*Stolperstein*) memorial was set in front of her former home.

107. *Hubert Sattlergasse 5:* Rudolf Löwy was the Jewish Community chairman after WWI, and he had his coal and fuel dealership here for many years before his death in 1935. He had originally established it as both a coal and raw leather dealership in the 1890s, but he gave up the leather trade in the early 20th century as his fuel business prospered. By the middle of the 1920s the business was doing so well that the *Iron Broom* called him the "Coal Baron" and accused him of trying to monopolize the business in Salzburg—while accepting generous advertising support from some of his non-Jewish competitors.

Rudolf's son Ludwig was running the business when the "Aryanization" process began in 1938. Ludwig tried to save the business by getting some non-Jewish friends to provide an "Aryan" front. The evasion was discovered and Ludwig was fined, as were his friends Rudolf Bernscherer, Josef Hübl and Karl Baumann.

The Nazis then "Aryanized" the business, turning it over to one of their supporters, Adolf Franz Herzog. The Nazis also "Aryanized" the cars of Ludwig and his brother Otto. Ludwig Löwy escaped to Palestine after he was released from *Dachau*, but returned to Salzburg in 1952 to resume his coal and fuel business. He followed his father's lead and became the president of the Jewish Community in the 1950s.

108. *Rainerstrasse 2:* *Rainerstrasse* was originally called *Westbahnstrasse*, and so this was the *Westbahnstrasse* 2 address of the Pollacks' antique business and apartment (see §69), the latter overlooking the Spa and *Mirabell* Gardens. In 1932 the street was renamed in honor of the 59th Infantry "Erzherzog Rainer" Regiment that was stationed in Salzburg.

Albert Pollak's business card.

Early in the 20th century Albert and Karoline Pollak's daughter, Käthe, operated her own second-hand business here until her marriage. In 1936 Albert Levi had a short-lived wholesale shoe business in the building. In addition, the attorney Dr. Josef Weiss and his wife lived here, as did Viktor Weinstein and his sister Else Steindler, who had an apartment upstairs and a shop downstairs. In 1938 all these properties were "Aryanized." At the time, the Pollak's apartment was still in the name of Albert's widow, Karoline, although she had long since moved to Vienna.

Rainerstrasse *2 in 1945, after the bombing.*

109. *Rainerstrasse 1 — The Spa:* The magnificent Spa (*Kurhaus*) was built in 1868 with a sauna, a steam room, and a heated bathing pool that was 36 feet long and 4-7 feet deep. The Spa also had several exercise rooms and numerous meeting rooms, and was one of the major attractions in Salzburg for many decades.

In August 1920 the Nazis held their Greater-Germany Meeting in Salzburg and a little known militant named Adolf Hitler gave a stirring speech at the Spa. It was so well received that the Salzburg Nazis invited him to return for the October election campaign, when he again spoke at the Spa. Here, on October 1, 1920, Hitler hinted at the "Final Solution" that was to come, saying: "The National Socialist Party is firmly committed to solving the Jewish Question with German thouroughness, right up to the ultimate consequences."

In November 1922 an associate of the City Theater scheduled a reading of the Austrian Jewish author Arthur Schnitzler's "Ballroom

Dance" (*Reigen*) at the Spa. A good-sized audience assembled for the reading, but was driven from the hall by a group of Nazi thugs while the police failed to intervene. When the *Iron Broom* threatened further disorders upon learning that a large party was scheduled here to celebrate the prominent Jewish matron Sarah Bonyhadi's birthday in 1923, the Spa management cancelled the reservation (see §78 and §111).

An American bombing raid badly damaged the Spa in 1944, and the ruins were finally demolished in 1953. It was replaced by several buildings: the modern Congress Center at the *Rainerstrasse* end of the Spa Park; the Hotel Sheraton next door; and the *Paracelsus* Swimming Pool and Health Center at the *Schwarzstrasse* end. Anybody who enjoys saunas in the nude (it is co-ed, but there is a separate women's sauna for the more modest) should definitely visit the fine facilities in the new Spa. There is also a large indoor swimming pool—bathing suits required. (In the summer, however, swimmers might rather enjoy the outdoor swimming pools in the *Volksgarten*, on *Sudalpinstrasse*, and near *Schloss Leopoldskron*, or even the fresh, cool waters of the *Königseeache*, just a few miles south of Salzburg, where it runs into the *Salzach* River, in the midst of lovely mountain views.)

110. Spa Park—Euthanasia Memorial: Inside this park, just inside the hedge along *Rainerstrasse* and near the *Mirabell* Palace, is a memorial to the two-hundred and fifty Salzburg victims of the so-called "Euthanasia" program. This is where the Nazis first developed their gas chambers at the end of 1939, before adapting them to mass murder and genocide after the "Euthanasia" program was shut down by public protests led by Catholic Bishops, including Salzburg's later Archbisop Andreas Rohracher.

111. *Rainerstrasse* 4: Adolf Pollak opened his second-hand business here in the mid-1890s, while his younger brother Albert was still located in the *Überacker-Palais*; and he remained at this location until his death in 1911, at age 83. His daughter Anna operated a second-hand shop here that was looted in the 1938 Crystal Night pogrom.

The insurance and commission agent Daniel Bonyhadi lived here for many years with his Strassburg-born wife Sarah and their children. He started off as a dealer in shoemaking supplies on *Bergstrasse* in the 1890s. Sarah had been a teacher and was the leader of the Jewish Women's Society, which had nearly fifty members between 1912 and 1930. She served as president from its founding in 1899 until 1931.

Sarah was also active in Red Cross relief activities during WWI. She was especially active for the group of Jewish refugees from the east who lived in a camp near Salzburg, at the foot of the *Untersberg* mountain near the cable car station in the village of *Grödig*. Her leadership qualities are reflected in her nickname, "the President."

Sarah and her sister were staunch German nationalists, so her Hungarian-born husband flew three flags from the flat on holidays: Hungarian, German, and Austrian. Sarah's sister even kept her savings in German marks, losing everything in the German inflation crisis of the 1920s. Sarah died in May of 1931 and only Daniel and his son Erwin were still registered here when the flat was "Aryanized" in 1938—the others having died or moved. Daniel moved to Vienna, where he died in 1939; Erwin, who was an accomplished opera singer, escaped to England, Switzerland, and finally the US.

Sarah Bonyhadi in 1921.

112. Franz-Josef-Strasse 4: In 1938 the apartment of Leo and Josefa Werner was here until it was "Aryanized."

113. Franz-Josef-Strasse 6: This shares a courtyard with Hubert Sattlergasse 5 and the Rudolf Löwy Coal and Fuel Company. Ludwig Löwy (see §107) and his wife Helene lived here until the business and the apartment were "Aryanized" in 1938. The apartments occupied by Klara and Heinrich Aninger (of Fischer and Aninger, see §13) and by Hans Aninger were also "Aryanized" here that year.

114. Franz-Josef-Strasse 1: The apartment of Lidia and Robert Löwy was here until it was "Aryanized."

Go up Rainerstrasse *on the left side to* Max Ott Platz. *Bear left onto* Ernest Thunstrasse *and* Plainstrasse. *Then go under the railroad causeway and turn left onto* Hans Prodingerstrasse.

115. Hans Prodingerstrasse: Formerly Slaughterhouse Street (*Schlachthofstrasse*), this thoroughfare was renamed after Hans Prodinger in 1953. Hans Prodinger was one of the first Salzburg State party chiefs of the Austrian Nazi Party, and was referred to in its newspaper as the "Salzburg Führer." On October 1, 1920, he shared the speaker's platform at a mass rally at the Spa with the newly popular Munich agitator, Adolf Hitler (see §38 and 109). After Hitler's fiery speech, Prodinger's was something of a letdown, so when they shared a platform again during the 1923 Austrian Nazi convention in Salzburg, Prodinger asked to speak first.

In the Spring of 1922, Prodinger was one of the creators of the successful electoral alliance known as the Christian-Nationalist Election Coalition. This was a united front of all the Antisemitic parties—Christian-Social, Farmers' League, and Nazi—against the Social-Democrats and "the Jews." Moving even closer to his new allies, Prodinger abandoned the Nazi Party in 1930 to join the Greater Germany Peoples' Party. Eventually he became a leader of the "Austro-

Fascists" in Salzburg. Although he never abandoned his Antisemitism, he did support the suppression of the Nazis after they attempted to seize power and assassinated Chancellor Dollfuß in 1934.

For his efforts, the Nazis considered him a traitor to the cause and targeted him for revenge. After the Annexation, he was arrested and sent to the *Dachau* concentration camp, where he was killed in September 1938. His martyrdom was widely used in the 1950s as a symbol of Austrian Nationalist resistance to the Third *Reich*, even though some Salzburgers questioned the propriety of honoring a former Nazi leader. A recent book on the subject listed *Hans Prodingerstrasse* as one of Salzburg's anti-fascist memorials, which seems like a strange claim given Prodinger's long career as a Nazi and "Austro-Fascist" leader.

116. *Hans Prodingerstrasse 19:* Immediately following WWII, a temporary synagogue was set up here. It remained in use for about a year, while the property remained in the possession of the Jewish Community until 1999.

Turn right at the next corner, onto Schwarzstrasse. *As you cross* St. Julienstrasse *to* Haunspergstrasse, *you can see the Elmo Theater a block away to your left.*

117. *Elmo Cinema:* At the beginning of April in 1951, the Elmo Cinema (*Elmo-Kino*) opened a showing of a new film by Veit Harlan, who had directed the vicious Nazi propaganda film "The Jew Named Süss" (*Jud Süß*). On April 3rd, the Jewish community of Salzburg took the lead in organizing a peaceful protest against this attempted rehabilitation of the Nazi director. Many Concentration Camp survivors from Salzburg took part in the protest. Altogether there were about sixty protesters in the theater when the police drove them out with their clubs. Some protesters were arrested while others were beaten and driven through the streets to the nearby Jewish Community Center on *Mertensstrasse*.

When the protesters tried to demonstrate outside the theater the next day, they were attacked by a mob that sent several demonstrators to the hospital and again drove the protesters to take refugee in the Jewish Center. The police stood by and did nothing, both during the attack and later when members of the mob outside the Center screamed "Come out you Jew pigs!" A victory of sorts was achieved when the American occupation authorities pressured the Austrian government into banning the movie.

Among the demonstrators on those two days was a Holocaust survivor from nearby Linz named Simon Wiesenthal. Wiesenthal went on to lead an effort to bring fugitive Nazis to justice. He wrote of his experiences in the death camps in his acclaimed book *The Sunflower*, and the Simon Wiesenthal Center in Los Angles was named in his honor.

118. *Haunspergstrasse 25:* This was the home of the Otto and Hilda Friedmann family from 1926 to 1938. Otto had learned the lumber business in Vienna from his uncle and moved to Salzburg in 1924 to set up a business here. Fortunately for the Friedmanns, Otto transferred most of his lumber business to a new firm he set up with a partner in Switzerland in 1937, though he continued to work from his office here on *Haunspergstrasse*. Otto was arrested in May 1938, but managed to convince the authorities that he was merely an employee of the Swiss firm that he had established. He fled into exile as soon as he was released. Hilda and the children stayed in the Salzburg house until it was "Aryanized" in November 1938. In 1940 the Nazis turned the *Haunspergstrasse* house over to an SS man named Dr. Kurt Lundwall and his wife Anna.

The Friedmann house in 1937, with Margaret and Fred Friedmann (front left).

    The Friedmanns' children were reunited with Otto in Switzerland, and later Hilda was able to join them. Yet even though Otto was part owner of a business in Switzerland, he was unable to get permission for the family to stay there. The Swiss have their own long history of Antisemitism, and proved very resistant to providing refuge for Jews in the 1930s and 1940s. Indeed, it was at their request that the Nazis marked the passports of German Jews with a large red "J" so that the Swiss could identify them at the border and keep them out. Eventually the Friedmanns made their way to a new home in New York City, where they started a new and successful life. Their son Fred was only twelve when they fled Salzburg, but fifty-five years later he said he still missed the good Salzburg bread.

Notice of "Aryanization" and eviction sent to Hilda Friedmann.

Fred began to make regular trips to Salzburg and has long served as the Austrian Honorary Consul in Buffalo, NY. In 2005 he and members of two subsequent generations of Friedmans came to Salzburg and stayed at the *Haunspergstrasse* address, in what is now the author's apartment. Fred said that the room he slept in here was the same room he had used as a child.

Fred and two more generations of Friedmans in front of the house.

Now backtrack a few yards to Mertensstrasse.

119. *Mertensstrasse 7:* This house contained the offices of the Salzburg Jewish Community in the late 1940s and 1950s. In the 1940s it also housed the offices of ORT (the Organization for Rehabilitation and Training), HIAS (the Hebrew Immigrant Aid Society), and other American-based Jewish relief organizations.

Continue on Mertensstrasse to Plainstrasse, turn left, and proceed to the next corner on the left.

120. *Purtschellergasse 12 (Plainstrasse 31):* This was the home of the Walter and Dora Schwarz family from the early 1900s through the 1930s. When they got married, Walter's family owned the largest clothing store in Salzburg, while Dora's family owned the largest clothing store in Innsbruck. Walter devoted most of his attention to the business, and built Schwarz's into a large department store and art gallery over the course of the 1920s. By the 1930s he was not only a partner in the Salzburg store, but had investments in England and Palestine, and had become half-owner of the Kraus and Schober store in Linz, and the *Fallenbiegl* Department Store in Vienna.

Walter had been wounded while serving in the Austro-Hungarian army at the battle of Isonzo in WWI. While he was hospitalized a fellow patient gave him some of Theodor Herzl's Zionist books to read. Walter and Dora's son Hugo said the books did not make much of an impression on Walter, but that when he passed them on to his wife, she became an ardent Zionist.

Dora Schwarz visited Palestine for the first time in 1924 and then convinced Walter to start investing in properties there so that they could emigrate someday. These included a sanatorium near Haifa and a business in Jerusalem. According to Hugo, his mother even became president of the Salzburg Zionist Organization (*Zionistische Ortsgruppe*), although the city directory listed his father, Walter, as president from 1931 to 1938. Several years before Dora emigrated to Palestine she had moved to Vienna with her two youngest sons, having become estranged from Walter. As Walter was still listed as president of the Zionist Organization long after she left Salzburg, it appears that he was more active in the organization than Hugo remembered. In the end, Walter was arrested and murdered by the *Gestapo*.

Dora and Walter Schwarz.

The couple ice skating together.

Return to Mertensstrasse *and turn left, looping around via* Ferdinand-Porsche-Strasse *to* Rainerstrasse.

121. *Rainerstrasse 31 — Grand Hôtel de l'Europe:* This was Salzburg's grandest hotel when it opened in 1865. Right next to the railway station, and with its own large park in front that opened onto fantastic views of Salzburg and its mountains, it retained its pride of place even after it was damaged by fire in 1928. In the 1940s it was used as a German Army Headquarters when the Army decided that the Hotel Bristol was too small. In 1945-1948 it became a reception center for DPs, even though it had been badly damaged by bombs. Demolition began in the early 1950s, and it was replaced by the current structure, the modern Hotel Europa. This hotel is far less grand than the predecessor, but the view from its top floor restaurant is no less spectacular, and well worth a visit.

Postcard of Hotel de l'Europe, 1908.

122. Südtiroler Platz — Nazi Victims' Memorial: Behind the Hotel Europa is the train station and *Südtiroler Platz*. On the west side of this plaza, under the trees opposite the station, is a strange structure that looks a bit like a concrete bus shelter, open on all sides and supported by only three columns. It is not very attractive, but if you go inside and look up at the ceiling you can read a long and moving inscription, in the name of the city of Salzburg, dedicated to each and all of the different groups of victims during the Nazi years:

> The City of Salzburg acknowledges and regrets that National Socialist crimes were committed here and that citizens of this city were among those guilty of these crimes. Among the victims of this barbarism were Jews, the psychologically ill and the handicapped, politcal dissenters, Sinti and Roma, homosexuals, artists, resistance fighters, prisoners of war and forced laborers, and other persecuted groups and individuals.

The remembrance of these dark years is a commitment to never allowing them to happen again. Lives of human dignity are based on the principles of democracy and human rights, on tolerance and the rule of law, and on solidarity and perseverance. These principles are not self-perpetuating, but must be defended against the development of an everyday Fascism, and must be achieved anew by every generation. Honoring the victims of yesterday means actively opposing all forms of Fascism, and struggling to protect human rights today.

Head back towards town, but turn right onto Ferdinand Porchestrasse, *and then left onto* Elisabethstrasse.

123. *Elisabethstrasse 1:* In the 1920s this was the home of the accountant Ludwig Pollak. He was the longtime head of the *Chevera Kadischa*, the Jewish Burial Society that owned the *Aigen* Jewish Cemetery, and he was the financial officer responsible for the *Lasserstrasse* Synagogue in the 1920s.

124. *Rainerstrasse 15-17:* Hermine Winkler and her nephew Hugo donated these two buildings to a pair of Jewish charities in 1937—the *Mensa Academica Judaica* and the *Israelite Institute for the Blind*. The two charities had little time to take advantage of their new properties before the Nazis "Aryanized" them in 1938.

Continue on Rainerstrasse *to* Max Ott Platz, *and turn right onto* Markus-Sittikus-Strasse.

125. *Markus-Sittikus-Strasse 14:* In the late 19th and early 20th century, Albert Levi from Württemberg and his sons Fritz and Julius had a large building on this block for their home and their textile and furniture wholesaling business. In 1886 Albert brought his cousin Adolf Jacoby (later of *Hubert Sattlergasse* 13) from Württemberg, and Adolf eventually became their office manager. The business went downhill after Albert died, and was closed in the 1920s. It is said that the older son then lost a fortune in the film business and that Albert's widow died a pauper in Vienna. In 1938 the Jewish wholesale agency of Dreifuss and Ottenheimer, which had moved into this address, was "Aryanized."

Continue to Schwarzstrasse *and turn left; then turn left again at* Auerspergstrasse.

126. *Auerspergstrasse 7:* Ernst Löwy lived here in the later 1930s, when he took over as the second head of the Salzburg branch of the Union of Austrian Jews (*Union Österreichischer Juden*).

Go back along Schwarzstrasse *to where it meets* Markus-Sittikus-Strasse. *Cross the street and go to the* Elisabethkai, *along the riverbank. Turn left and go towards the* Müllner Steg *footbridge, until you are opposite the large* Müllner *Church across the river.*

127. *The Burning Ground:* This is where Salzburg's Jews were burned to death on July 10, 1404. Archbishop Eberhardt presided, while soldiers under the command of his brother Sigmundt, who was captain of the guard, killed about seventy men, women, and children—that is, all but three of Salzburg's Jews over age ten (see §128).

One version of the tragedy places the burning "on the saddle point of the gravel, right across from *Mülln,*" while other records put it on the *Müllner* Church's grain field, across the river from the church. It is unlikely, however, that the grain field itself would have been used, since a fire would have destroyed a growing crop in July; but the gravel-covered bank between the field and the river would fit both descriptions, as the *Müllner* Church's grain field would have included the land around the Spa and at least that part of the Spa Park below the Rose Hill. The riverbed has been altered over the past six-hundred years, and the site would now be some distance away from the river, most likely between this spot and *Schwarzstrasse.*

Now cross the Müllner Steg *footbridge—not, of course, without stopping to appreciate the view of Salzburg. Jog to the right, and go up the steps to* Müllner Hauptstrasse. *Turn right onto* Müllner Hauptstrasse, *and take the first left leading to the church, noting also the chapel across the street at* Müllner Hauptstrasse 6.

128. *Müllner Church (Müllner Kirche)*: Just as an earlier Roman settlement here had been a suburb of "*Juvavum,*" *Mülln* was a suburb of Salzburg in the Middle Ages. Its ancient church, renovated after a fire in 1148, was the site of a break-in by a thief in 1404. Trying to avoid a death sentence, the thief claimed that "the Jews" had paid him to break in and steal consecrated Host (communion wafers) for them to desecrate. He said they wanted enough wafers to be able to provide them to other Jewish communities in the region. This accusation led to the judicial murder by fire of the Jews of Salzburg (see §6 and §127) and Hallein after some "confessions" were extracted through torture. In a later renovation of the church, an enameled window was installed in the sacrament house telling the story as it was remembered by the Christians of *Mülln*:

> Notice how the Jews of Salzburg, as was their custom, contracted with a pusillanimous Christian who, thinking only of money and failing to consider the fate of his soul, agreed to steal the body of the true God [the consecrated Host] from this place for 350 Hungarian gulden. The man climbed in through the roof of the Chapel of our Beloved Lady in *Mülln* and stole all the holy *Corpus Christi* and gave it to the Jews. He said that one of them had told him that they had arranged with other Jews from far and wide to share God's promise fulfilled through the Christians [i.e., Christian salvation].
>
> When the Christians heard of this great evil they took it to heart and rounded up all the Jews of Salzburg and Hallein in an hour and then searched for the Host in the houses on the *Judengasse,* looking for it in books and under the stairs where they had hidden it, but could not find it. They were punished with the fire on the saddle point of the gravel, right across from *Mülln.* At this time Erberhardt von Neuhaus was Archbishop here, his brother

Sigmundt Neuhauser was Captain, and the Judge was Niclas Ziegl. This happened on the 14th of July in the year 1404 after the birth of Christ [actually, July 10].

The current *Müllner* Church may actually be further up the hill than this early building, since the current structure dates from a 1439-1453 reconstruction, which may have involved a move. If there was such a move, the present chapel at *Müllner Hauptstrasse* 6, which was used as a leper asylum after the 1439-1453 reconstruction, would have been the location of the original church in 1404.

The oldest view of "Miln," showing both church and chapel, from a 1553 woodcut.

After leaving the church, go up to the left until you reach the road heading up Mönchsberg. *Follow this road up to the front of the Hotel* Mönchstein.

129. *Hotel Mönchstein—the Medieval Burial Ground:* The original Jewish cemetery was here in the 14th and 15th centuries. It was still known as the Jews' burial ground several centuries later when an observatory for the university was built in the old stone tower that was here in 1654. In 1770 a palace, called *Schloss Mönchstein*, was built on the site of the stone tower, and it was reported that the construction workers found many human remains when they dug the foundations. Today *Schloss Mönchstein* has been enlarged as the Hotel *Mönchstein*, and there is no sign of the old cemetery.

Go back through the Mönchsberg *gate and turn left on the path that goes along the north side of* Mönchsberg. *Go to the second lookout point, after passing through the wall. There you will see a clear view to the north, west, and southwest.*

130. *Mönchsberg Lookout—DP Camp Beth Bialik, 51 Klessheimer Allee:* Looking northwest you can see, just east of the railroad tracks, an industrial area which was the site of a labor barracks built by the Nazis in 1938-39. During the war years, part of it was also used as a military clothing factory and a women's work camp and prison. When it was re-opened as a DP camp in August of 1946, it was renamed *Beth Bialik* by its residents, after the Hebrew "national poet" of Polish Jews. With around 2,500 residents it was greatly overcrowded, but they still managed to make a temporary life for themselves here. Their more than three-hundred and fifty school-aged children were organized into four "collectives" (*kibbuztim*), one for each major national group in the camp. They had a House of Study (*Bet Hamidrash*) for religious instruction, a drama circle that put on plays, and a reading room which carried both German and Russian newspapers. By 1949 all of *Beth Bialik's* Jewish residents had left, and the camp was closed.

131. *Mönchsberg Lookout—the Gold Train Warehouses, 55 Klessheimer Allee:* On the northwestern edge of Salzburg, just west of *Beth Bialik* and across the railroad tracks, there was an army barracks and storage depot built in 1941 for the German *Wehrmacht*. After the War, American occupation forces used it as a barracks and storage depot for an armored regiment until 1951, calling it Camp *Kleßheim*. Thereafter, for the next few decades, it was an Austrian Army facility called the *Struberkaserne*. In 2003 the Austrian government proposed turning it into a detention camp for asylum seekers, a proposal resisted by the Salzburg authorities. At last report the government has decided to sell the land for a housing development.

Jewish interest in this site begins with the March 30, 1945, arrival of a train from Budapest, carrying forty boxcars of valuables that had been seized by the Nazis from the Jews of Hungary. These included art, gold, jewelry, silverware, fine china, porcelain, rugs, and religious items. While much of the gold was in the form of coins and jewelry, there was also a considerable amount of dental gold, removed from the bodies of Jews murdered in various extermination camps. The Nazis had intended to keep the loot away from the advancing Soviet armies by moving it into Germany.

Later called the "Gold Train," twenty-four of its boxcars ended up in the hands of the US Army when it organized the occupation of Austria. The contents were quickly identified as having been stolen from Hungarian Jews. At the time, on the basis of perhaps only two-thirds of these boxcars, the contents were valued at between fifty and a hundred and twenty million dollars. This included sixty chests of jewelry and 200-300 chests of silver tableware.

Despite the great value of these goods, the warehouses into which they were deposited here were poorly secured, and it was reported that many items were simply looted. In addition, low ranking officers like Lieutenants Kenneth P. Fischer and Richard L. Jewitt requisitioned some items for their personal use, especially silverware, glassware, and china. Other items of value were appropriated by higher ranking officers of the US Army, as when General Harry J. Collins, Commander of the Rainbow Division, requisitioned forty-five settings of china and silverware, glassware for ninty people, thirty sets of tablecloths, and sixty sets of bedding. "The General," it was stipulated, "desires that all of the above listed items be of the very best quality and workmanship."

Word of the fine quality of the materials in the Salzburg warehouses resulted in still other requisitions by American generals and high-ranking officials stationed in Austria and Germany. Indeed, no effort was made to prevent them from simply shipping the valuables along with their personal effects when they returned home to the US.

Rather than meet its obligation to return the property to its owners, the US Army later decided to classify the valuables as "captured enemy property." As a consequence, sacks of gold coins were transferred to the US Austrian Currency Section, and later turned over to the Austrian government, along with gold that was legitimately part of the Austrian treasury. The bulk of what remained was shipped to New York in early 1948, and thousands of the most valuable items were auctioned off to the highest bidder. The rest was distributed to various Army bases in the US.

The story of the Gold Train finally became public when it was included in a 1999 report by the Presidential Advisory Commission on Holocaust Assets in the United States. Hungarian Jewish survivors and their heirs filed suit for the restitution of their stolen property in 2001; and in 2002 the US District Court rejected the government's claim of immunity, allowing the case to go forward.

A legal settlement providing for a US government apology and a 25.5 million dollar payment to needy Hungarian Jewish Holocaust survivors was approved by the Court in September 2005. On October 11 of that year, the US Department of Justice issued the following apology: "The United States regrets the improper conduct of certain of its military personnel and seeks in this settlement to provide meaningful assistance to those Hungarian Holocaust survivors still living, who qualify as financially needy."

Looking to the left, you will see the Salzburg Airport.

132. *Mönchsberg Lookout—Salzburg Airport:* After the establishment of the State of Israel in 1948, Jewish refugees could go to Israel legally and easily. On the 25th of November, the first flight carrying eighteen Jewish DPs directly to Israel left the Salzburg Airport. That December, nine-hundred more followed.

Under military guard, Jews board the first plane from Salzburg to Israel.

From Mönchsberg *go down to the* Müllnerbräu *entrance; continue across the street and to your left, as you pass the* Müllner *Church.*

133. *Müllnerbräu—Camp Mülln:* This was one of the first camps for DPs in Salzburg, established in the summer of 1945. A transit camp for 200-250 residents, it was set up inside the famous *Müllnerbräu* beer hall, home of *Augustinerbräu* beer. It was a short-term stopping place for DPs en route elsewhere (mostly to Palestine), and most residents stayed here less than seventy-two hours. By 1947 the flow of DPs had slowed, and Camp *Mülln* was closed.

This was also the first Salzburg headquarters of a Jewish group called the *Bricha* ("the Flight"), which was responsible for organizing a massive illegal migration to Palestine that passed through Salzburg. It is estimated that between 1945 and 1947 the *Bricha* enabled the emigration of 63,000 Jews through Salzburg, financed mostly through a Jewish organization called the Joint Distribution Committee.

Abba Gefen (left) and Marko Feingold (on the right) with three friends.

Abba Gefen, a member of the Zionist Revisionist youth movement, *Betar*, was the commander of the *Bricha* in Salzburg. Marko Feingold, a Holocaust survivor originally from Vienna, was the local leader who worked closely with Gefen to facilitate the transports. Feingold, as he himself recalled, was able to get several trucks from the Salzburg authorities by reminding them that if they continued to refuse his request, thousands of Jews would remain in Salzburg. US occupation officials also provided some clandestine assistance, their priority being to get DPs out of their zone of control: Gefen recalled that the US motto was, "Out with the DPs." Jewish-American servicemen provided even more assistance.

Marko Feingold, sometime after his release from Buchenwald in his KZ uniform.

For the first year or so, the *Bricha*'s trucks transported the refugees on back roads across the Italian border with French occupied Tyrol. In 1947, however, the British Government got the French to close the border in an attempt to stem the flow of refugees to Palestine. Feingold then used a far more strenuous route over the mountains in the southwestern part of the American occupied province of Salzburg, where it shares a short border with Italy. In the summer of 1947 some five-thousand DPs were transported in groups from Salzburg to a guesthouse high in the *Krimml* Valley, above its famous waterfall. Usually waiting there until dark, they then made their way, without lights, up the valley another three-thousand feet, to a moutain pass at an elevation of 8,500 feet. There they crossed into Italy and were met by additional trucks when they reached the main road down below.

Bricha DPs crossing the high pass in 1947.

In June 2007 there were a series of commemorations of this exodus on the occasion of its 60th anniversary. A large group of participants, including a handful of veterans from the original crossing, retraced the steps of the *Bricha* across the pass and into Italy.

Part III

❖❖❖

Some Additional Sites

(less centrally located)

134. *Rennbahnstrasse 11:* The home of Otto and Helene Scheck before it was "Aryanized."

135. *Ignatz Rieder Kai:* The Gypsy memorial, dedicated in 1986 (see §49).

136. *Mayburger Kai 38:* The home of Rabbi Dr. Samuel David Margulies, his wife Rosa, and their two daughters before it was "Aryanized," and they fled to England.

137. *Wiesbauerstrasse 9 and 12:* While the offices of attorneys Dr. Franz Grün and Dr. Julius Pollak were at *Dollfußplatz* 8 (see §72), they lived at *Weisbauerstrasse*, numbers 9 and 12, respectively, Pollak with his wife Frieda, and Grün with his wife Ilse. Pollak owned both of these properties when they were "Aryanized." One was taken over by the SA for a Brigade headquarters, and the other was taken over by an SS unit. Pollak and his wife fled to Montevedeo in 1938.

138. *Schwarzparkstrasse 11:* This is the home and synagogue of Rabbi David Nussbaum. A *Lubavitcher* rabbi from New York, he served as the rabbi for the *Lasserstrasse* Synagogue from 1990-2001. After leaving the *Lasserstrasse* Synagogue, he and his Israeli-born wife moved to this location with their three sons. They had a small synagogue built onto the house, and often offered *Shabbas* (Sabbath) meals as well as religious services for Jewish visitors. In 2006 Mrs. Nussbaum and the children moved to Vienna so that the children could attend a Jewish school, obliging Rabbi Nussbaum to curtail somewhat the services and hospitality of *Schwarzparkstrasse* 11.

Organizations of Interest with Contact Information

Salzburg Jewish Cemetery — Aigen
Uferstrasse 47
A-5020 Salzburg
Open by appointment, contact the Synagogue at:
Tel. (43) 662 87 2228
Email: *office@ikg-salzburg.at*

Synagogue and Jewish Community of Salzburg
Lasserstrasse 8
A-5020 Salzburg
Tel. (43) 662 87 2288
Email: *office@ikg-salzburg.at*

Rabbi David Nussbaum
Congregation *Beth Zedek*
Chabad Lubavitch
Schwarzparkstrasse 11
A-5020 Salzburg
Tel. (43) 662-87-565 or (43) 664-7944-194
Email: *DavidNussbaum770@hotmail.com*

Center for Jewish Cultural History
Residenzplatz 1
A-5010 Salzburg
Tel. (43) 662 8044 2961
Email: *zjk@sbg.ac.at*

(Note: when dialing in Austria, substitute "0" for the country code "43.")

Bibliography

(Note: a much fuller bibliography, including German titles, is given in the original German edition of this *Guide*.)

Browning, Christopher R. *The Origins of the Final Solution: The Evolution of Nazi Jewish Policy, 1939-1942.* Lincoln, NB: University of Nebraska Press, 2004.

Bukey, Evan Burr. *Hitler's Austria: Popular Sentiment in the Nazi Era, 1938-1945.* Chapel Hill, NC: University of North Carolina Press, 2000.

Hsia, R. Po-chia. *The Myth of Ritual Murder: Jews and Magic in Reformation Germany.* New Haven, CT: Yale University Press, 1988.

Katz, Jacob. *From Prejudice to Destruction: Antisemitism, 1700-1933.* Cambridge, MA: Harvard University Press, 1980.

Kertzer, David I. *The Popes Against the Jews: The Vatican's Role in the Rise of Modern Antisemitism.* New York: Alfred A. Knopf, 2001.

Leeson, Daniel N. "Mozart, the Jews and Late 18th Century Austria." *Mozart-Jahrbuch 2002*, pp. 155-167.

Lewy, Guenter. *The Nazi Persecution of the Gypsies.* Oxford: Oxford University Press, 2000.

Steinberg, Michael P. *The Meaning of the Salzburg Festival: Austria as Theater and Ideology, 1890-1938.* Ithaca, NY, and London: Cornell University Press, 1990.

Thurner, Erika. *National Socialism and Gypsies in Austria.* Edited and translated by Gilya Gerda Schmidt. Tuscaloosa, AL: The University of Alabama Press, 1998.

Trachtenberg, Joshua. *The Devil and the Jews: The Medieval Conception of the Jew and Its Relation to Modern Antisemitism.* New Haven, CT: Yale University Press, 1943.

Zweig, Ronald. *The Gold Train: The Destruction of the Jews and the Looting of Hungary.* New York: Morrow, 2002.

NOTES

1. Stefan Zweig: *Die Welt von gestern: Erinnerungen eines Europäers*, 392-93.
2. Marko M. Feingold (ed.) *Ein Ewiges Dennoch: 125 Jahre Juden in Salzburg*, 201; quoted from Josef Kaut, *Festspiele in Salzburg*, 350.
3. Feingold, *Ein Ewiges Dennoch*, 7.
4. Stefan Zweig, *Die Welt von Gestern: Erinnerungen eines Europäers*, 329-330.
5. Ibid., 428-29.
6. November 12, 1985; in Feingold, *Ein Ewiges Dennoch*, 380.
7. Christopher R. Browning, *The Origins of the Final Solution*, 186.

Index of Entries

51 *Klessheimer Allee*	129
55 *Klessheimer Allee*	129
Alexander Moissi Straße	53
Alter Markt	18
Alter Markt 12	19
Auerspergstraße 7	126
Bebel Memorial Plaque	24
Bergstraße 8	94
Burning Ground	126
Café Bazar	68
Camp *Hellbrunn*	56
Camp *Herzl*	103
Camp *Judah*	64
Camp *Mülln*	13
Cathedral (*Dom*)	40
Cathedral Square (*Domplatz*)	43
Chiemseehof	38
City Theater	91
Corner of *Makartplatz* and *Dreifaltigkeitsgasse*	80
DP Camp *Beth Bialik*	129
Dr. *Adolf Altmann Straße*	58
Dreifaltigkeitgasse 3-5	80
Elisabethstraße 1	125
Elmo Cinema	118
Euthanasia Memorial	115
Faberstraße 7	111
Faberstraße 8	107
Faberstraße 11	110
Festival Buildings (*Festspielhäuser*)	31
Franciscan Street and Cloister	37
Franz Josef Kaserne	103
Franz-Josef-Straße 1	117

Franz-Josef-Straße 4	117
Franz-Josef-Straße 6	117
Franz-Josef-Straße 8	110
Franz-Josef-Straße 12	110
Furtwängler Garden	28
Getreidegasse	25
Getreidegasse 9	25
Getreidegasse 14	27
Getreidegasse 21	27
Getreidegasse 24	28
Getreidegasse 26	30
Getreidegasse 27	30
Getreidegasse 34	30
Gold Train Warehouses	129
Grand Hôtel de l'Europe	123
Gypsy Camp *Leopoldskron-Maxglan*	60
Hallein	41
Hans Prodingerstraße	117
Hans Prodingerstraße 19	118
Haunspergstraße 25	119
Haydnstraße 2	102
Haydnstraße 5	103
Haydnstraße 10	109
Hotel Bristol	93
Hotel *Mönchstein*	128
Hubert Sattlergasse 5	112
Hubert Sattlergasse 7	111
Hubert Sattlergasse 13	107
Ignatz Rieder Kai	137
Inner Stone Gate (*Innerer Steintor*)	69
Jewish Cemetery	54
Jew's Mountain (*Judenberg*)	47
Judengasse	12
Judengasse 12	17

Judengasse 15	12
Judengasse 17	17
Kapitelplatz	40
Kapuzinerweg 5	72
Klessheimer Allee 51	129
Klessheimer Allee 55	129
Kranzlmarkt 1	23
Kranzlmarkt 2-4	21
Kranzlmarkt 4	19
Lager Glasenbach	51
Lasserstraße 6	97
Lasserstraße 8	97
Leopoldskron Palace	57
Leopoldskron-Maxglan	60
Linzer Gasse 5	76
Linzer Gasse 20	94
Linzer Gasse 26	95
Linzer Gasse 28	95
Linzer Gasse 48	96
Linzer Gasse 52	96
Linzer Gasse 53	96
Makartplatz	80, 83
Makartplatz 1	84
Makartplatz 4	93
Makartplatz 7	84
Makartplatz 8	84
Markus-Sittikus-Straße 14	125
Mascagnigasse	56
Max Reinhardtplatz	31
Mayburger Kai 38	137
Medieval Burial Ground	128
Mertensstraße 7	122
Mirabellplatz 6	104
Mönchsberg Lookout	129-32

Mönchsberg 18	63
Mozarteum	89
Mozart Square (*Mozartplatz*)	9, 45
Mozartplatz 5	10
Müllner Church	127
Müllnerbräu (Brewery, Beerhall, and Garden)	132
Nazi Victims' Memorial	124
New Palestine	75
New Residence	45
Nonnberg Cloister and Church	48
Nonnberg Lookout	47-57
Old Market (*Alter Markt*)	18
Paris-Lodronstraße	101
Paris-Lodronstraße 2	105
Parsch	75
Peterskeller	37
Plainstraße 31	122
Platzl	66
Platzl 2	69
Platzl 5	69
Purtschellergasse 12	122
Rainerstraße 1	114
Rainerstraße 2	112
Rainerstraße 4	115
Rainerstraße 15-17	125
Rainerstraße 31	123
Rennbahnstraße 11	137
Residence Square (*Residenzplatz*)	43
Residenzplatz 1	45
Richterhöhe Lookout	57-61
Riedenburg Barracks (*DP Lager Riedenburg*)	51
Robert Jungk Platz 1	71
Salzburg Airport	131
Schallmooserhauptstraße 6	97

Schallmooserhauptstraße 6a	97
Schatz Passage	24
Schloss Leopoldskron	57
Schrannengasse 10	103
Schwarzparkstraße 11	137
Schwarzstraße 1	68
Schwarzstraße 3	68
Schwarzstraße 5-7	84
Schwarzstraße 13	85
Schwarzstraße 14	69
Schwarzstraße 22	91
Schwarzstraße 24-28	89
Sigmund Haffnerstrasse 9	24
Spa Park (*Kurhaus Park*)	115
Spa (*Kurhaus*)	114
St. Andrä Quarter	102
St. Peter's Church	37
St. Petersbezirk 5	40
State Bridge (*Staatsbrücke*)	66
State Theater	91
Stefan Zweig Villa	72
Steingasse	69
Steingasse 2	69
Steingasse 4	69
Steingasse 18-21	69
Steingasse 31	70
Steingasse 43	71
Südtiroler Platz	124
Toscanini Court	36
Town Hall Square (*Rathausplatz*)	25
Überacker-Palais	80
Uferstraße 47	54
Universitätsplatz 3	31
Universitätsplatz 9	31

Vierthalerstraße 8	101
Waagplatz	11
Waagplatz 6	12
Wiesbauerstraße 9 and 12	137
Witches' Tower	101
Wolf Dietrichstraße/Paris-Lodron-Straße	101
Wolf Dietrichstraße 2	96
Wolf Dietrichstraße 14	102

www.ingramcontent.com/pod-product-compliance
Lightning Source LLC
Chambersburg PA
CBHW072148160426
43197CB00012B/2302